P9-DDS-561

# Jim
# <u>Elliot</u>

## WOMEN OF FAITH SERIES

*Amy Carmichael*
*Corrie ten Boom*
*Florence Nightingale*
*Gladys Aylward*
*Hannah Whitall Smith*
*Isobel Kuhn*
*Mary Slessor*

## MEN OF FAITH SERIES

*Borden of Yale*
*Brother Andrew*
*C. S. Lewis*
*Charles Finney*
*Charles Spurgeon*
*Eric Liddell*
*George Muller*
*Hudson Taylor*
*Jim Elliot*
*Jonathan Goforth*
*John Hyde*
*John Wesley*
*Martin Luther*
*Samuel Morris*
*Terry Waite*
*William Carey*

*John and Betty Stam*

# Jim
# Elliot
## Kathleen White

# BETHANY HOUSE PUBLISHERS
MINNEAPOLIS, MINNESOTA 55438

Grateful appreciation to Elisabeth Elliot Gren for providing photographs of her late husband which were used to paint the cover illustration.

*Jim Elliot*
Kathleen White

Library of Congress Catalog Card Number 90–55457

ISBN 1–55661–125–0

Copyright © 1990
All Rights Reserved

First published in Great Britain by Marshall Morgan and Scott Publications Ltd.
Published by Bethany House Publishers
A Ministry of Bethany Fellowship, Inc.
6820 Auto Club Road, Minneapolis, Minnesota 55438

Printed in the United States of America

# 1

A spontaneous cheer broke out from the four young fellows as the fragile Piper aircraft bounced down on the crude landing-strip. From the open cockpit, Nate, the pilot, leaned out and called to them exultantly, cupping his mouth with both hands so that the sound would carry down the beach to them. "They're on their way at last!"

Slapping each other on the back and shaking weather-beaten hands, coarsened and calloused by months of toil, they made their final arrangements with mounting excitement. Those on their way were none other than a group of men from the savage Auca tribe, headhunters from a Stone Age environment. Cut off from twentieth-century civilization, they lived deep in the rain forests of Ecuador. Occasionally stories of their primitive lifestyle and murderous attacks on neighboring Indians filtered through to the world outside, yet they themselves were largely an unknown quantity.

But it was just to meet superstitious people like these and bring to them for the first time the life-changing message of God's love that these five young men had studied and sacrificed for many years. Now, clustered together and joined by Nate who had sprung lightly out of the aircraft and come bounding across the white sand towards them, Pete, Ed, Jim and Roger planned the last details of their campaign.

"I'll get Marj on the radio," decided Nate, and straight away, made contact with his wife, cranking up the handset. Guardedly and still using code words, he nevertheless made sure the message was received clearly. "Pray for us—we'll be on the line at four-thirty. Maybe we'll have some news for you then."

After a quick lunch, the friends filled in the time by making a model house and jungle on the sand to show the Aucas how they could help the white men if they wanted them to come and join their community. By clearing the immediate thick fringe of forest trees and creating a reasonable airstrip, they would make access much easier for the little Piper plane and the many loads of necessities which it would fly in.

For the past few days, the five missionaries had slept in makeshift tree houses with an improvised kitchen set up on the ground under the trees. At best, that could only be a temporary arrangement. Their imaginations raced excitedly ahead of the present situation. "We can bring in more food and medical supplies once we've established a base. Just think what we can do for the Aucas when we are settled in—if they allow us to do so." Happily discussing possible plans for the future, they all eagerly awaited the arrival of the ten tribespeople Nate had spotted earlier in the day.

We rest in Thee, our Shield, and our Defender,
We go not forth alone against the foe.

Strong in Thy Strength, safe in Thy keeping tender,
We rest on Thee, and in Thy name we go.

Through the small clearing their deep voices combined joyously in singing once more what had become almost a theme song for them throughout "Operation Auca." At last the moment was here for which they had prayed, planned and hoped during many years of preparation, through frustrations and encouragements. What thrilling stories would they be able to tell their wives when they next made radio contact? How soon would the women in turn be able to beam out the news to their parents, prayer partners and home churches who had lovingly and sacrificially supported them in their enterprise?

But that call was never made. Back at Shell Mera, Marj Saint and Olive Fleming hovered anxiously over the radio set, willing it to crackle, to emit some signal, however feeble, that would convey some short message from the men. Making excuses for the delay they still stayed close to the set but it remained steadfastly and chillingly silent. What could possibly have gone wrong?

Not one of those young fellows would have claimed to be the leader of the group. They all worked in close harmony, each contributing his own special expertise towards the realization of their project. Nate Saint, for instance, proved invaluable to their success. Trained as a pilot and employed by Missionary Aviation Fellowship, he ferried them over Auca territory in the first exploratory flights, enabling them to make contact and leave gifts and tokens of their friendship and goodwill from the safe distance of the plane.

Yet of the five by far the most detail is known about Jim Elliot. His wife, Elisabeth, after his untimely death, collected together as many of his letters and papers as possible. In addition, from 1948 to the end of 1955, Jim wrote down his thoughts, aspirations and quite often his frustrations in his diary, beginning as a college student and ending as a full-fledged missionary. The first few recorded words read, "What is written in these pages I suppose will someday be read by others than myself. For this reason I cannot hope to be absolutely honest in what is herein recorded. . . ."—a frank admission of his human frailty, which he was the first to acknowledge.

In his biography *Shadow of the Almighty*, Elisabeth used many passages from his letters and the journal. Later, when publishing his diaries in full, she admitted, "There were those who felt despair on reading the biography, for Jim seemed larger than life, too holy, too single-minded to be believed. I felt that such readers had not read very carefully, for the flaws, the flesh, the failures were there." She had not deliberately concealed any facet of his nature but the selection could not possibly give the whole picture. However, when the complete journals finally appeared in print, it was Elisabeth's wish that readers would appraise Jim for his true worth. Without glossing over his faults and weaknesses, she wanted as well to show his dedication as a true servant of the Lord Jesus. So, a very clear portrait of Jim eventually emerged, "warts and all," but all the more convincing for that.

With a surname like Elliot and a Christian name like James, it would seem more or less inevitable that somewhere back in the family tree Jim could claim Scottish ancestry. And indeed it is not necessary to look too far back because in the mid-nineteen hundreds his Elliot great-grandparents sailed from Scotland to start a new life in the small village a hundred miles west of Toronto. Conditions were difficult in the border country at that time, and no doubt, like thousands of their fellow-countrymen, they hoped they would be able to gain a livelihood more easily by starting again in a land full of promise and opportunities.

Jim's father Fred was a grandchild of this pioneering couple but his mother came from different stock and an even more distant country. Her forebears in Switzerland were also lured to Canada by the potential of that country, richly endowed with natural resources. Significantly, it was in church that Fred first set eyes on Clara and he lost no time in paying attention to her. They were married in 1918 after Clara had graduated, making their first home in Seattle for four years.

Fred had suffered a setback to his formal schooling as a young teenager, "I'm afraid you'll have to leave your studies and help with chores around the house," his father told him reluctantly. His mother was delicate and couldn't cope on her own. In those days on a stock farm, both the owner and his wife were tied to an inexorable yearly calendar of duties around the estate with few modern gadgets or pieces of machinery to help the various processes. Fred shouldered that burden without grumbling.

Clara was more fortunate than her husband because she had been able to complete her studies at a chiropractic college. This stood her in good stead as she used her training to work for their first four years together, rather unusual for a married woman just after World War I. No doubt this made a great difference to the household budget. With Fred working as an evangelist, money would have been tight without Clara's regular contribution of her professional fees.

Even when the children began to arrive, she still continued to practice but made sure the children did not suffer from neglect. Their needs were given priority and she always worked in a room of the family home so the children were in constant touch with their mother. Robert was born in Seattle in 1921, but the other three, Herbert, Jim, and Jane were born in Portland, Oregon, in 1924, 1927 and 1932 respectively.

It must have been quite heartwrenching for the parents to leave Seattle, with its beautiful water location, and move south to the next state, Oregon, to live inland in Portland, but Clara's father owned a house there which they took over. However, the children enjoyed compensations like beach picnics down on the coast during the summer months. With only a spread of eleven years between the youngest and eldest, they never lacked for companionship in outdoor pursuits.

During the winter months, sledding on mountain slopes provided a source of excitement. The children were also encouraged to grow fruit and vegetables and learn how to deal with animals. Much of their expertise was acquired from their grandparents' farm. Obviously Fred and Clara wanted their children to grow up with a wide range of experience, leading a well-balanced life. "All work and no play. . . ." certainly didn't apply to them.

Hobbies added an extra dimension to life. Each child chose his own. Jim spread his leisure time over several different interests: model-making, stamp collecting and reading. Early on he demonstrated a love for color and beauty, but equally for adventure and speed when he tore through the town on his bicycle at a breakneck pace! He would be remembered for that long afterward.

Fred, as an evangelist, might have been tempted to give them too stringent a religious training but he was too wise a parent for that. He read the Bible every day to them and expected them to attend church and Sunday school from school-age upward, but the children weren't brought up in a purely negative way: "You can't do this, people will talk if you do that." When old enough, they were encouraged to make their own decisions.

Perhaps the most important decision in his life was made by Jim at the age of six. "I'm saved now," he told his mother after a meeting one night, and he would talk about it quite naturally to his young friends. It would have been quite easy for him to adopt a holier-than-thou attitude if his parents hadn't handled all their children so carefully. To them, their faith was an integral part of everyday life, not a code of rules to be put on like a best suit to be worn in church on Sundays.

Although very much an individual, there were certain qualities of spirit he inherited from both his

parents. Jim was never afraid of hard work, physical
or mental. He was also never blessed with a surplus
of money. As a student at college, he had to earn what
he needed by taking on extra jobs. It probably did
much more for his development than a handout from
wealthy parents would have done. A close family tie
existed between the immediate six members of the
Elliot family which also extended outside to the
whole clan. So many of Jim's letters which have sur-
vived illustrate this point. These proved an invaluable source of information when Elisabeth was com-
piling a record.

Full of energy and with a zest for living, Jim
reached his teenage years eager for new experiences.
Not all his ambitions were accomplished. When at
sea on the way to South America with a another missionary, he confided in his journal, "All the thrill of
boyhood dreams came over me just now . . . watching
the sky die in the sea on every side. I wanted to sail
when I was in grammar school and well remember
memorizing the names of the sails from a diction-
ary. . . ." But that was denied him in Portland. Perhaps he thrilled to stories about the sea from his father who had lived close to it during his time in
Seattle.

At that stage, there was very little to set him apart
from other boys in his class and certainly nothing to
suggest that one day his name would ring round the
world in an epic story. There must have been
hundreds of other lads like him even in his own
home state of Oregon, keen for adventure and to taste
the thrills that life had to offer. Yet the early commitment to God had put its own mark on Jim. Hardly

aware of the significance of the step he had taken at first, he nevertheless remained true to the commitment to Christ he had made as a small boy, and as he grew physically so did his desire to serve the Lord.

# 2

At fourteen Jim changed schools and became a student at Benson Polytechnic High School. There he chose architectural drawing as his main subject. Color, shape and design had attracted him as a primary scholar and several of his early drawings ended up on the walls of the classroom for display. But it wasn't just for his formal studies that he gained a reputation. Editorials written by him appeared in the school newspaper. He also took a leading part in many school dramatic productions and won a great deal of applause. "I wish you'd take acting up as a career," urged a teacher. "You show a good deal of talent which would be worth encouraging if you decided to concentrate on that."

Allied to this love of theater was his performance in delivering speeches. He belonged to a public-speaking club in which he often participated. On one occasion he upset the president by refusing to speak on behalf of a political candidate because of his personal conviction that, as a Christian, he couldn't be involved in war or politics. He did, however, offer to explain his reasons to the club, an offer that was politely turned down because the president realized it would afford Jim a golden opportunity to deliver a stirring Gospel message to the whole debating society!

Yet when President Roosevelt died, he did rise to the occasion and give a speech in honor of his memory which was dubbed by a tutor "the finest I've ever heard from a schoolboy."

Conditions weren't too easy for young Americans in school during Jim's High School years. As time passed, gasoline rationing began to bite as a result of wartime restrictions, and many were the hilarious incidents which befell Jim and his friends in their efforts to thumb a ride. Sometimes it was just a routine journey home after school hours, but occasionally a crowd of young fellows set off on camping expeditions, heavily weighed down with packs and essential equipment. Sportingly Jim took part in football matches with more enthusiasm than skill, which caused his friends a good deal of amusement.

He also gained their respect, apart from becoming involved in extra-curriculum clubs and activities, by "nailing his colors to the mast." They may have not shared his views but they could not fail to notice a small Bible carried on top of his pile of textbooks, nor the fact that he always made a point of saying grace before eating in the student cafeteria.

At the end of a long day, chores still remained to be done at home, caring for the animals or general maintenance jobs. He certainly stood no chance of becoming "so heavenly-minded that he was of no earthly use." Carrying out practical duties was an equally essential part of his training, as was his personal evangelism, although Jim wasn't averse to roping in his friends to share in his tasks if he could diplomatically persuade them!

Girls appeared more than a little interested in him, but he was rather cagey about their advances. Elisabeth wryly passed on a comment which was related to her by Dick Fisher, a close friend of Jim's from grammar school. "Domesticated males aren't much use for adventure," he warned Dick. Although another interest of Jim's was reading poetry and later composing verses himself, he didn't waste his energies in writing romantic odes to the opposite sex. Girlfriends did not figure largely in his program. It wasn't until he met Elisabeth and got to know her well over a period of years that he could quote from Shakespeare about "the marriage of true minds." He could have expanded the reference, from the sonnet:

> Let us not to the marriage of true minds
> Admit impediment. Love is not love
> Which alters when it alteration finds
> Or bends with the remover to remove.

But all that lay a long way ahead. Physical attraction was also to be a recognized force in his relationship with Elisabeth. He freely admitted it in frequent jottings in his journals. He was a perfectly normal, natural man, but the factor of primary importance was the union of thought and common purpose they had learned to identify and acknowledge in each other.

During his four years in high school, he derived a great deal of fun from exploits with his friends. Sometimes that involved unsavory garbage collecting with his older brother Bert, and then removing and trading in stacks of empty bottles at the supermarket afterwards. That, however unpleasant, brought them very welcome extra pocket money. Jim's parents were remarkably liberal in allowing him to go off camping with friends for several weeks on end, but he in turn respected their scruples by trying to make sure he didn't miss weekend services at the Gospel Hall. Letters from his father while he was away on trips were always highly treasured. Jim valued his father for his consistency in the "things of God" throughout his life and no doubt this had a formative influence on his development.

Wartime brought another problem for young men. Although too young to be personally affected by the draft, Jim nevertheless had to think it through for himself. Finally he decided he could never be anything other than a conscientious objector on this issue, following the example of Christ, "If my servants were of this world, they would fight." That was his interpretation of the Scriptures which he stated unequivocally, although not imposing his opinions on others.

It was a courageous stand to take at a time when patriotic fervor was at its height and he stood the risk of being misunderstood on account of his principles. He also took a stand when he refused to buy a ticket for the school dance. For Jim again, it was only the right thing to do. "I'm in the world but not of it," he quoted, and nothing would move him on that point. Because of his uncompromising attitude on topics like these he put his own popularity and success as a natural leader on the line, but in spite of this he was made vice-president of his class in his senior year.

Finally the time came when he had to leave home for further studies. He had been well equipped by his parents to face the outside world. They had given him a solid base of love and security, a feeling that each one of the family mattered tremendously to them and to God. To their children they had tried to pass on a respect for traditional virtues such as obedience and honesty, and had taught their three sons and only daughter to discipline themselves and not allow themselves to become too self-indulgent.

Home was always a fun place to be, with friends made welcome whenever they turned up on the doorstep. Over the years, missionaries from many different countries called and stayed there, giving Jim a chance to find out more about them, and question them more closely than he could have by just hearing them give a talk illustrated by slides at the local church.

Now it was time to move on. As usual, no parental pressure was put on Jim to make a certain choice. He was expected to make his own prayerful decision.

The year 1945 became a watershed both in the history of the world and in Jim's own personal life. Global warfare had at last come to an end. In May an armistice was signed in Europe between the allied forces and Nazi Germany. By August the total collapse of the war in the Far East followed the horrific devastation after the first atom bombs to be used in modern warfare had been exploded over Japan. After six years of horrendous conflict, the weary world sighed for peace and normality. For many it naturally became the moment to resume their former way of life, return to families or the advancement of careers and studies interrupted by their years in the armed services. They were the fortunate survivors. Many millions of their generation and their parents' also had lost their lives either on the battlefields, under the crumbling ruins of bombed-out cities or in the gas chambers of Auschwitz, Dachau or Ravensbruk.

This welcome release from the specter of war which had haunted the universe for such a long period came at a natural break in Jim Elliot's studies. His four years of high school completed, he had to take the next step towards his training for adult life. A bewildering array of courses and opportunities lay ahead of him. Which option would he choose?

"Jim's aim was to know God," Elisabeth stated categorically in his biography. So any decision about his training and final goals must be influenced solely by his commitment to Christ and Christ's claims on his life. If this sounds pious and unnatural for a young man of eighteen, it gives the wrong impression. Jim had simply sorted out his objectives earlier in life than most, not because of a premonition of his death or a desire to impress others with his piety.

Following Jesus was no ego-trip for him. He didn't deliberately choose to set himself up as a Christian folkhero, although that is what he eventually became. Two years later, at the age of twenty, he would be praying, "Lord make my way prosperous, not that I achieve high station, but that my life may be an exhibit to the value of knowing God." It's quite commonplace to pay glowing tributes to someone after he has died, but Jim's daily diary when he was still very much alive bore truthful witness to the sort of Christian he really was.

Jim opted for Wheaton College, Illinois, and it was there he was to spend the next four, formative years. It would take him a long distance from family and friends. From living near the west coast of America, he had to take a journey eastward of nearly two thousand miles to a state lying at the southern tip of Lake Michigan. Air flights were fairly infrequent and expensive in those days and hadn't yet superseded train travel. But there were times when Jim couldn't even afford the railroad and thumbing a ride provided the only means of transport home for vacations.

On one memorable occasion he arrived at Portland after twenty different rides, taking seventy hours in all to cover the route. His cheerful comment was, "I've $1.32 in my pocket and we beat the slow train! Haven't we a wonderful Lord!" That journey involved sleeping on a "smelly couch" in a back room and driving with a sailor whose language was particularly offensive. But Jim made it and enjoyed the experience, making a joke of his adventure on his return.

Money, or rather the lack of it, would always characterize Jim's arrangements. It wasn't a priority with him, but when he became particularly hard up he was always prepared to earn some by his own efforts. His partnership with his older brother Bert in garbage collecting was an amusing example, but it kept him solvent. As long as he lived at home finances weren't too much of a problem; by the time he reached college he was faced with the prospect of providing fees every term. No one person had promised to back him. Gradually the whole amount came in by means of part-time work, a friend's help and a scholarship he was awarded. "Thank the Lord," was Jim's reaction, learning how practical was His faithfulness.

He never regreted choosing Wheaton, which was a small Christian college twenty-five miles west of the great city of Chicago. It had achieved a sound academic reputation and presented a formidable challenge to all the students who joined the campus. Five years earlier another young American Christian whose name would become familiar throughout the world, arrived as a freshman. He too was compelled to work his way through college with no support from his father. For three hours every afternoon, Billy Graham could be seen crashing through the streets of Wheaton, moving goods and hauling them in his old-fashioned yellow truck, his princely salary being fifty cents an hour. Like Jim, he picked his future wife, Ruth Bell, from his fellow-students but was able to marry her within three years, not encountering so many obstacles as Jim and Elisabeth to delay their wedding.

By the time Jim arrived at Wheaton, Billy had already left and had not yet made his mark on the nation as an evangelist. However, the atmosphere and influences they both encountered there must have played their part in molding these two men of God and in helping them decide where their paths lay in the future. Billy's debt of gratitude to his college prompted him to set up The Billy Graham Center at Wheaton to train "key church members from the Third World," to provide a Laymen's Bible Training Institute and a vast library with all the archives connected with his huge organization.

Jim's memorial would be less tangible, less visible, but the effect of his ministry, although short, was far-reaching and of tremendous consequences in the evangelical world. But none of this was in his mind when he entered Wheaton for the first time in 1945. He was dedicated and singleminded, although it would be considerable time before he knew for certain how God was going to make use of his talents in the future.

# 3

*I*t wasn't until the start of January 1948 that Jim began to write down his thoughts and meditations daily in his journal. So for the first two years at Wheaton, the only information about him comes from letters to his family and verbal recollections of his friends, which fortunately proved remarkably vivid. He had that effect upon people.

Although a host of choices awaited the new students on enrollment, Jim restricted both his choice of subjects and his leisure-time activities to dovetail with his wholehearted consecration to his Christian commitments. That didn't mean that he stuck out from the rest as an oddity. His cheerful smile made him many friends on the campus. Sometimes he took part in a Saturday afternoon football match, although often he tried to discipline himself to stay in on Saturday nights to prepare himself mentally for the Sunday communion service.

This discipline showed up too in his choice of wholesome food in the college cafeteria, all geared to toughening his body for the missionary work ahead. He preferred a fresh, natural diet rather than highly seasoned and sophisticated dishes. Of course his choice was also governed by the amount of money in his pocket. Never being very affluent, he had to pick the cheaper items on the menu.

He also regarded himself as steward of his time. That meant an early wakening by the alarm clock to fit in time for prayer and Bible study at the start of the day. "None of it gets to be 'old stuff,' for it is Christ in print, the Living Word," he wrote. This thorough knowledge of the Bible would prove an asset later on when he took on pastoral duties in America and afterwards at mission stations overseas as he shared it with others.

Reading the Bible wasn't just a daily routine task for Jim to be fitted in between meals, personal duties, leisure time and socializing. A significant quotation in *Through Gates of Splendor* underlines his deep love of the Scriptures. In a letter to his parents just after he became sufficiently familiar with the New Testament Greek, he expressed himself feelingly. "Today I read the story of the Cross in John 19 for the first time in the original. The simplicity and pathos made me almost weep; something which has never occurred in my English reading." This preoccupation with language would stand him in good stead later on when he was trying to master a few phrases of the Auca tongue, which had never been written down. How Jim longed to be able one day to translate parts of the Bible for people who had no knowledge of the Gospel message!

Absence from home made his heart grow, if not fonder, more appreciative of all his parents efforts on his behalf. Probably he felt it was easy to take them for granted while still living in the family home, but at college he slowly came to realize how they had helped to establish him as a young Christian. One particular phrase stands out when he refers to a " . . . father-preacher who has not spent so much time rearing other people's children that he hasn't had time for his own." Jim hitchhiked back to Portland for the whole of his first summer vacation from college.

At the start of his second year, Jim found himself less starry-eyed about "the acquisition of academic knowledge" but even more drawn to the pursuit of knowing Christ better. That he counted of much greater value. Other decisions had to be faced which he shared with his family in letters. A job arose which offered him free tuition for a year, but after wrestling with his conscience he turned it down because it would interfere with his mainstream studies and involve him in what he considered time-wasting social activities.

Fred Elliot was anxious for his son to derive the greatest possible benefit from his years at college because he himself had been forced to break off his studies to help on the farm at home. While Jim agreed with his father, he was also afraid of just trying to gain an academic reputation and being sidetracked from the main purpose of his training. Perhaps he was becoming slightly disenchanted with intellectual studies for their own sake. Jim quoted from 1 Corinthians 8:1, "knowledge puffs up," in one letter to his parents, ". . . education is dangerous . . . I am beginning to question its value in a Christian life. I do not disparage wisdom—that comes from God, not from Ph.D's." Had Jim been familiar with *The Screwtape Letters*, he would have heartily agreed with C.

S. Lewis when he wrote, "What we want, if men become Christians at all, is to keep them in the state of mind I call 'Christianity and . . . ,' " and then Lewis added a list of diversions to mainstream Christianity which would divert people from the real purpose. Lewis puts these words into the mouth, or rather the pen of the devil Screwtape, writing to his nephew Wormwood to help him in his task of preventing a seeking soul from becoming an ardent Christian. Jim feared anything that might "turn aside the hearts of many here on campus from a humble life in the steps of the Master."

He found his schedule quite demanding and asked for prayer to be enabled to keep up with his exhausting program. Characteristically, though, he made time to practice wrestling and was even once included in the varsity team, feeling that the discipline would harden his body and toughen it for missionary service later on, despite his mother's natural misgivings! In no sense, however, did Jim despise education. He remained grateful for the opportunity to go through the college courses, only begrudging the time spent on some rather abstract theories when he could have been concentrating on "the things of God."

Prayer sessions with several of his housemates became very precious to him—"the first fruits of Glory itself." When the Student Foreign Missions Fellowship visited colleges in that area, he joined a team of speakers and gave a ten-minute talk on the Holy Spirit in missions. In assessing his first two years at Wheaton, he acknowledged the joy that his close personal relationship with Jesus had become and he testified to the power of prayer. "This to me is real Christianity, when fellows pray and see miracles worked on campus the following day."

Always he was conscious of time passing quickly and therefore anxious to accomplish as much as possible. During the first two years at Wheaton he became aware that the Lord was challenging him personally to go out as a gospel preacher. Mission statistics which he had copied out in college weighed heavily upon him. Once possessing such telling facts and figures, there was no way he could square his conscience to remain in the United States, even in full-time Christian service. To quote just one, "There is one Christian worker for every 50,000 people in foreign lands, while there is one to every 500 in the United States."

At first he had no clear indication where he would serve, but took the opportunity to see missionary life in the raw during the 1947 summer vacation. A friend, Ron Harris, had parents working in Mexico so the two students hitchhiked down there. During his six-week stay Jim began to study Spanish and even took a children's meeting towards the end with his very limited vocabulary. Two significant phrases stand out in a letter to his parents, "Mexico has stolen my heart," and "Missionaries are very human folks . . . simply a bunch of nobodies trying to exalt Somebody."

By the end of his visit he felt drawn to working in Latin America, yet at that stage he had no idea how it would work out. His next major decision was made for him as funds earmarked for him came in and enabled him to stay at college for a further two years. His interest in Spanish continued and he chose Greek as his major to enable him to understand the New Testament in greater detail. This, he deemed, could also have a possible spin-off later in assisting him when he wanted to translate the Bible into a strange, unwritten tongue.

Having sorted out a fairly tough assignment for himself, Jim knuckled down to a concentrated program of study, prayer sessions, and physical exercise with precious little leisure time. Then life took an unexpected twist which could totally have disrupted his tight schedule if he had allowed it to do so. Sitting across the aisle from him in the ancient history class was a girl who shared an almost identical timetable— a rare occurrence in such a large college with so many different options. They apparently didn't make any immediate impact upon each other and were probably unaware of their close proximity for a while, until one day Elisabeth came to the conclusion that this rugged fellow Elliot must be her brother Dave's teammate from the wrestling squad.

It was earlier on in that same year, 1947, that Elisabeth had confided in her diary, "longing for someone to love but perhaps the Lord wants me only for himself." Thirty years later Elisabeth revealed that remark to her reading public when she published a book titled *Passion and Purity*, giving advice to teenage girls on how it was possible to be deeply in love yet keep oneself pure from sexual sins in accordance with God's commandments.

From this point they began to chat occasionally and Jim even asked her for a date which Elisabeth later broke. This caused quite a stir among their fellow students because Jim had so far resisted feminine charms. What did Betty have to deflect him from his self-imposed discipline? They looked on her with a new respect and curiosity. Not that Jim was an anti-social being, far from it, but God's claims on his life were given top priority. Other distractions, however natural and desirable, had to take their place in line.

Elisabeth Howard and her brother Dave were both students at Wheaton over the same period with the two young men in the same class year. It was hardly surprising that two members of the Howard family had chosen to train at Wheaton Bible College. Elisabeth explained in her book *These Strange Ashes*, an account of her first year as a jungle missionary, "My parents had been missionaries, I was born in a foreign country, and when we returned to the United States, we lived close enough to New York to be always meeting boats with missionaries on them and seeing people off for faraway fields." So her early missionary impressions weren't just gleaned from books, but firsthand from people with years of experience behind them.

A chance to get to know each other better materialized when Dave invited Jim home for Christmas. Jim wrote enthusiastically to his parents describing the family—Phil and his wife Margaret, Elisabeth just twenty-one, Dave, Ginny, a teenager, followed by Tommy, thirteen, and Jimmy, seven. The Howards took to Jim immediately and he fit in quite naturally helping with jobs around the house and sledding with the younger members.

Elisabeth enjoyed late night discussions with him on a variety of subjects. When they returned to Wheaton for the spring term, they found themselves spending more time together, usually over study, and several months elapsed before Jim confessed to a growing personal interest in her. It wasn't that he had been impervious to her attractions from the start, but he needed to wait for God's timing to declare what would prove to be the most important relationship in his life.

Soon after this he began recording his thoughts and impressions on passages from the Bible in a daily journal. This habit lasted until the end of December 1955, a few days before his death. Jim was afraid that he might be tempted to present himself in too favorable a light, with a view to public acclamation in the future, but on the whole his observations were honest and from the heart. Elisabeth, too, showed courage in publishing the complete journal in 1978, having already used extracts in *Shadow of the Almighty*. Encouraged by the many hundreds of letters she received and conversations with a broad cross-section of the Christian public, twenty years after his death Elisabeth revealed the whole man by releasing all the extracts. Jim's reputation in no way suffered as a result.

Characteristically he prayed in the first month of writing, "May I burn up for Thee. Consume my life, My God, for it is Thine. I seek not a long life, but a full one like Yours, Lord Jesus." The last entry of all included the words, ". . . I have been very low inside me struggling and casting myself hourly on Christ for help." Jim never considered that he had "arrived" or attained Christian perfection, just as Elisabeth was at pains to present an all-round picture of him not just as a man of God but a school champion wrestler, consistent honor student and amateur poet as well.

Somehow with all his other activities, Jim always found time to write to his brothers and sister, and also to his parents. In one letter home he described how he had narrowly escaped injury from a railroad accident. God must have had a purpose in this. "Certainly He has a work that He wants me in somewhere." No one could have guessed then that in a few more years He would suddenly claim that life. "Pour out my life as an oblation for the world," Jim offered.

Elisabeth's approaching graduation brought matters to a head. Realizing that she would soon be leaving Wheaton, Jim took her for a walk one evening and both declared their love for one another. But this relationship wasn't going to take the usual predictable course of engagement, sparkling ring and marriage. First of all, they had to wait for God's seal of approval and His time signals, even, if necessary, denying themselves the pleasure of planning shared lives together later.

It wasn't an easy decision, both being normal young people and physically attracted to each other. Elisabeth inserted a sentence in the journals. "Agreeing . . . the matter was too big for us to handle, we decided to pray about it separately." Several diary entries around this date indicate Jim's state of mind, " . . . have had trouble in concentration," and "Wept myself to sleep last night after seeing Betty off at the depot. Wistful all day today in spite of outdoor exercise."

Happily, they were both of one mind that Betty's

life had been "placed on the altar of sacrifice to the Lord." Yet Jim confessed that he cherished hopes that God would give her back to him eventually. In writing this Jim felt challenged that he was anxious to take from God something that had primarily been dedicated to Him. But he was only human. "I must go on asleep (in the deep sleep of Adam) until God sees my need of Eve," he wrote. "Fix my heart wholly, Lord, to follow Thee . . . not to touch what is not mine."

# 4

Diary entries on the subject of Elisabeth ceased to appear for a while, almost as if Jim had left the whole matter with the Lord and had peace about it. Another more strenuous enterprise filled his thoughts and energies for the immediate future. After attending Wheaton summer school, Jim set off with a gospel team consisting of Dave Howard, Roger Lewis and Verd Holstern under the auspices of the Foreign Missions Fellowship. Their journey took them through many Midwestern states from Michigan to Montana and they spoke at a variety of places—youth camps, schools, churches, and summer conferences. At one stop early on in the campaign, they felt discouraged by the smallness of the place, but the next day in his diary Jim wrote, "... God is leading surely and we are not to despair if things seem small or commonplace." Three weeks later on August 14 he recorded, "Good day of stirring and heart-searching in Bemidji, Minnesota."

They worked on a fairly tight schedule. In a letter to his mother Jim confessed to typing even while they were traveling. He also found time to read Hudson Taylor's life story during that month. He mentioned it twice in letters so no doubt it had a significant effect on him afterwards—a classic missionary biography of a giant of a man who set out to take the Gospel to China by faith alone, without any appealing for funds. Jim's letters usually contained an assortment of news items first of all but usually led on to spiritual matters. One flowed quite naturally from the other; it didn't appear as though Jim was writing with an eye to publication later on. He probably didn't even realize how much his letters were treasured and hoarded by members of his family. Thankfully they were and later these formed a unique source of information and gave a clear insight into what he was thinking at that time.

Then, with a poet's eye, Jim might suddenly switch to an appreciation of the wonders of nature: "I think I have never so enjoyed a sunset as the one we saw last evening." Later, toward the end of the trip he wrote, "The beauty of the West cannot be written; so high it is, it can hardly be enjoyed in its fullness."

He managed to spend a few days in Portland before returning to college for his last year. A long descriptive letter to his brother Bert, who was away from the family gathering in Arkansas, hinted at his indecision about future plans. ". . . I have felt a shifting burden from Latin American interests to Oriental fields, more particularly India . . . the sad neglect of the North American assemblies weighs heavily upon me. We have . . . two brethren from North America, in a country of 400,000,000!"

Jim's constant references to "assemblies" and "brethren" indicated he belonged to and worshiped with the Plymouth Brethren, small groups of evangelical Christians with no central organization or affiliation. Every male member was encouraged to take part in the services but no priests or pastors were ordained.

In September 1948 Jim began his final year at college. Early on in the term Elisabeth visited him. They had made a pact with each other that they wouldn't write during their three-month absence but even so Elisabeth noted, "Our love for one another had grown." He felt close enough to her to invite her to read his first completed journal and also wrote to his parents to share his feelings for Elisabeth. In case his mother and sister became excited at the prospect of a wedding in the air, he frankly divulged that they had even contemplated going through life unmarried, if God so required it, but he added the comment, "I can hear Ruby (Jim's sister-in-law) laughing." How difficult it was to explain something he didn't even understand fully himself! Marriage to Betty would be the fulfillment of many dreams and yet he could not enter into any life-long contract until he had the Lord's complete assurance for this important step in his life. Fortunately Betty herself understood what a struggle was raging within him even though it placed a strain upon her also.

It must, however, have been a relief to her when Jim decided they should start writing to each other again although their letters were few and far between. The content of Jim's more than made up for their infrequency, absolutely honest and full of spiritual meat as well as personal comment as they were: "There is within a hunger after God, given of God, filled by God. I can be happy when I am conscious that He is doing what He wills to do within."

His feelings fluctuated. Sometimes he was conscious of a "flood of peace within" as he sought God's face. At other times he bemoaned his coldness and lack of fruitfulness for the Lord. A letter of thanks to his mother written on his twenty-first birthday highlighted the two main concerns in his life just then. He had registered as a Conscientious Objector and wondered if he might be called up for some form of non-combatant service or whether he might soon accomplish his personal goal and reach the mission field. He was torn between undergoing a longer training period and rushing out to try to save millions who were passing away to a Christless eternity. He was also concerned about the need to learn a tribal language as well as Spanish so he could become more effective in reaching the Indians.

Occasionally a few lines of verse he had composed himself were included in his letters. At other times he recreated particular scenes of beauty which had caught his imagination: "I wish I could describe the color . . . I can't remember enjoying beauty in the full as just now." This sense of well-being permeated his whole soul that autumn. "He is giving me such good things I wonder I could want more." Recurring both in his journal and letters are constant references to his meditations on the Scriptures: "They that wait upon the Lord shall renew their strength."

Christmas 1948 found him apologizing to his parents, because instead of sharing in the family festivities, he planned to be present at the Student Missionary Convention at Illinois University.

In a letter to them Jim appealed to his father as man to man to give him some advice on setting out for the mission field. Then, in a loving rebuke to his mother whose maternal fears and reservations were only natural, he begged, ". . . please let's not have any more of this talk about staying home, telling people of the 'need.' I feel as if I haven't got any excuse whatsoever to let a body such as you have given me get fat leaning on pulpits."

Jim was very unlikely to put on any flesh at all with his hectic program embracing not only a heavy workload of academic study for his final examinations, but also the many extra duties that arose from his presidency of the Student Foreign Missions Fellowship. Nor was he ever likely to yield to maternal misgivings about the dangers of missionary life while he still carried those oft-quoted statistics around in his wallet: "Sixty-four percent of the world have never heard of Christ. Five thousand people die every hour."

> From subtle love of softening things,
> From easy choices, weakenings,
> Not thus are spirits fortified,
> Not this way went the Crucified.

Thus wrote Amy Carmichael, a physically weak woman who nevertheless took on the extremely dangerous task of rescuing Indian children from the clutches of evil temple authorities, and was also a prolific authoress.

Jim quoted these lines in his journal and later other verses from Amy Carmichael's writings. He must have sensed in her a kindred spirit, like-minded with the same goals and determination.

He also broke out into verse in his journal from time to time as when, for instance, he wanted to stress to people the personal reality of a God "of the here and now."

> But I found God in the sidewalks
> The backyard, and our upstairs,
> . . . My Christ stands not in a synagogue
> With a beard and a long white gown,
> But I know Him in the grocery store,
> He rides our car downtown.

In between all his commitments, Jim found release in sharing ordinary family activities: "Thanksgiving at Auntie's with the annual turkey and trimmings," and two months later a trip home to Portland for his brother Bert's wedding. His inner conviction that this would be the last complete gathering of the Elliot clan was proved right later, but it wasn't spoiled by sadness at the time. Rather, his links with his father were reinforced as he wrote later to Elisabeth, "His theology is . . . so real and practical . . . that it shatters every 'system' of doctrine I have ever seen. He cannot define theism but he knows God. We've had some happy times together."

There were times when Jim became impatient with assembly diehards: "I feel I'm getting a bit cynical about these smug, powerless P.B.'s. When it is good it is very, very good, but when it is smug, it is horrid." Needless to say he never included his father in this category, though he came from a Brethren background. His father was a real man of God and walked very close to the Lord. It was hypocrisy and self-inflation that riled Jim.

He started the New Year of 1949 with one positive result from the Missionary Convention. The Lord had at last made it quite clear to him about his service abroad. With a deep sense of relief he wrote to Elisabeth about the outcome, "I am quite at ease about saying that tribal work in the South American jungle is the general direction of my missionary purpose." He also told her, ". . . the Lord does not want me seeking a wife until I have His definite sign." This Elisabeth graciously accepted, even offering to forego the letter-writing if it proved a hindrance to him but Jim refused to break off the correspondence. "God has led us together in writing."

Probably because of his Brethren background, Jim had worked out for himself a strict code of conduct to which he had adhered fairly rigidly. With more maturity, he came to realize that it was creating an artificial barrier between groups of students, those more "spiritual," like members of the Foreign Mission Fellowship, and those more interested in sports. He called this experience his "Renaissance" or new birth and it enabled him to take part in many activities he would have shunned previously. He lightheartedly mentioned dressing up in Victorian costume for Centennial Day, and wrote of a wrestling banquet when he was billed to sing "The Shooting of Dan McGrew" and "The Cremation of Sam McGee." After enjoying fellowship on an outing with other students, he commented somewhat wistfully, "I wish now that I had understood how to deal with them. Seems like I've only caught on myself this spring."

Sympathetically he wrote to his parents as his brother Bert and wife Colleen were leaving. "Bet you felt it hard, Mom and Dad, and the Lord knows why." Twice he comforted them with more lines from Amy Carmichael's poems. She had experienced that emotional tug-of-war in leaving her mother and friends when sailing away from the shores of England on a long voyage to the other side of the world, and so knew the cost of the sacrifice firsthand.

In 1978 when the journals were published, Elisabeth dedicated them to Bert ". . . who went to Peru where he has been a missionary for thirty years in the High Andes and the tropical forests." It was Bert who was quite willing to stay at home praying for Jim, but God in His inscrutable purposes saw fit to prolong Bert's term of service abroad while He cut the thread of Jim's life.

Three years after Bert's departure when he himself sailed for Ecuador, Jim was able to enter into his parents feelings again. "I surely praised God for the valiant way you both took my going. . . . All I understand is that it must be very keen, deep and closely linked with all that this life involves for you. I pray . . . asking 'the help that is from God' for you both."

Several other outings and camps enabled him to get close to other students in his new sense of liberty. "The Lord has freed me from many things—good, consecrated attitudes, priggish little laws whereby I used to govern my conduct," he wrote. "I experience new fellowship, new freedom, new enjoyment." In his journal he acknowledged, "I love to be with a gang. Fellowship with the gang is enticing fun."

Yet he was always aware of the possibility of overindulging his sense of fun and afraid of talking down to the very students he was trying to help. It would be very easy to inflate his own ego by searching them out to minister to them.

The name of Ed McCully crops up quite casually at this stage, first as a senior member who won the national oratory competition in San Francisco and later broke the bread and gave thanks for the cup at a camp communion service. Jim described him as "a good buddy of mine" who also worshipped at a Brethren assembly. Later on he was to play a significant role in the Auca project.

Mr. and Mrs. Elliot must have enjoyed their trip to Wheaton to witness Jim graduate with highest honors, and it also must have helped to alleviate their natural sense of loss at Bert's departure. Jim drove back with them and his sister Jane after the ceremony, relieved to be another step further in reaching his goal, but sad to leave many of his old friends with whom he had studied for four years.

He had formed no long-term plan for his future but had promised to help his brother Bob to build a house for him and his wife. "I feel that three months' building would prepare me more for the missionfield than another three months in the books." Later he was to prove the value of this practical work when he found himself called upon to construct buildings in much more primitive conditions.

The trip home took several weeks as Mr. Elliot stopped off to preach at various places along the route. Jim's entry in his diary upon arrival in Portland reads, "Home at 7272 at last. Mingled feelings of 'not belonging' and thanksgiving for all God's grace these last few days—these past four years, in fact." That was written on July 8, 1949.

# 5

*T*his feeling of "not belonging" probably per-
sisted for a while. Glad to be back with his
parents whom he held in the highest regard,
Jim must nevertheless have felt himself in limbo. Big
brother Bert had already achieved his ambition to set
out for the mission field with his wife. For the immediate future Jim possessed no clear blueprint, neither had he received confirmation from the Lord con-
cerning marriage to Elisabeth. Being sent out by an
established missionary society was easier and
quicker for a candidate than gaining the support and
approval of "the Brethren" for a venture. The same
selection machinery did not exist, nor were there
mission headquarters staff to speed the arrangements.

But Jim, being who he was, was not one to be
deterred by considerations such as these. He recognized them—he certainly didn't hide his head in the
sand, but he faced up to the challenge. In December
of the previous year, knowing a little of what lay
ahead, he had written to the family, "The uncertainty
of the next year adds its sobriety to my thinking, but
for all these things, I would have no cause to call

upon the Remover of Hindrances. Banish your fears; my soul is glad in God, though I tend to aggrandize the difficulties and fail often to give glory to the Great Solver thereof.''

It could have been difficult too in returning to worship solely in Brethren assemblies after the greater freedom of the independent groups at Wheaton, but Jim was convinced of the rightness of their pattern of meeting on New Testament principles even if he did have critical things to say about the pomposity and blinder vision of some of the older, entrenched members of the movement. At its best, he could talk feelingly of "the simplicity and powerful beauty of the New Testament fellowship," and he always acknowledged his debt to his early training in the things of God.

Elisabeth called this chapter in her biography of Jim "The Test of Free Time." After a highly structured program, Jim was faced with the problem of organizing his time constructively on his own initiative.

Just eight days after his return, a journal entry reads, "All day at the hall, washing and preparing it for painting— maybe next week." Then, a week later, "Painted part of the hall today. Restless to do other things more directly related to the Lord's work." In the same paragraph, he longs for a friend who will play David to his Jonathan. He must have keenly missed the companionship of other students to mull over spiritual matters together and also to join in light-hearted social activities. Most young people of his age in Portland would probably be out at work during the day. The end of college always brings a sharp division in a graduate's life, but for Jim it was a particularly acute contrast with little money, no immediate plans and the necessity to prove himself in the work at home before the Brethren would sanction his going overseas.

Still he enjoyed sharing the work-load with his father even if the jobs seemed slightly trivial like painting the house, cleaning up the meeting-hall and fixing the car. And he still felt a conviction that this waiting time was of the Lord, which helped him to be at peace about it. A snag occurred over the plans for his brother's house which needed to be sorted out by the city authorities first, so he couldn't start on the more challenging construction work as he had hoped originally.

A comment on July 16 gives a hint of the strain he must have been undergoing in adjusting. "Much in exercise about personal holiness which I dreadfully lack . . . argued with Mom at supper before the whole family tonight." Perhaps Mom was acting a little too protectively toward her son now that he had returned for a while to the family nest, and Jim was feeling edgy and unsure of himself. Yet this period of waiting was not to be wasted. Later on Jim would be thankful he had learned to work cheerfully on seemingly insignificant projects, to be sensitive about other people's feelings and to fit in as a member of the team—all essential when he was eventually thrust out into a pioneer missionary environment. In that situation there would be no room for a self-inflated egotist or a learned Bible scholar who was afraid to get his hands dirty.

Jim continued to get inspiration from reading, not

only the Bible, but David Brainard's diary, which he mentions more than once. Then again he derived "comfort from A. C." (Amy Carmichael). Jim possessed an empathy with Amy. She, too, had suffered frustrations before finding her true niche in missionary service. Bad health constantly dogged her early efforts. It prevented her being accepted by the C.I.M. in the first place. Then she was compelled to leave Japan after serving only fifteen months there. A short stay in Sri Lanka was followed by a trip back to London. Even when she finally reached India, where she spent the rest of her life, she was hindered by illness in the early stages.

Jim possessed a fine physique. He had kept his body in shape by his wrestling training but there were days, as in Amy's experience, when he found the waiting time irksome. As he broke out into writing verse from time to time, so he enjoyed reading Amy's poems. She had the knack of compressing truths into a few lines. Her verse was honest and unsentimental although it came from the heart.

At the beginning of September Jim was heartened to listen to a report of the work in Jamaica. "We need no missionaries here," declared the speaker, and this was because the national believers were working hard themselves to build up the local churches. This must have been music in Jim' ears. He never visualized himself as an immovable figurehead but rather a pioneer worker who would eventually hand over the running of the church to people from the tribe who had been saved. Jim was not to realize this ambition in his lifetime but fortunately there were like-minded Christians to carry on in the same way to establish local churches. There was no paternalism in Jim's approach to the unreached peoples of the world, only a desire to live and to share.

September brought a welcome change in Jim's routine when Elisabeth arrived for a visit on her way home from rural missionary work in Alberta. Elisabeth's first impressions were of a comfortable house which had been extended to meet the needs of a growing family. Fruit trees and flowers were planted on the sloping hillside and masses of blooms decorated the glassed-in porch so that rich colors and fragrant scents predominated.

Mrs. Elliot was as welcoming as the invitation she had sent Elisabeth—a motherly figure beside her rugged husband. Jim took time off to drive Elisabeth to the Pacific coast of Oregon, to climb Mount Hood and canoe along the Columbia River—all outings which he must have enjoyed many times before with the family but which took on a new beauty and significance when shared with his beloved. Elisabeth experienced the genuine warmth of the family's welcome. She had come as a result of many invitations and felt a rapport with both Jim's parents.

"Strange, but oh such happy days," Jim confided in his diary, and then after Elisabeth's departure, "She has been gone one hour. What thunders of feeling I have known in that short time . . . leaving her is terrible." Yet he had still received no concrete answer to his problem. Every time he saw Elisabeth he felt more closely drawn to her, but there was the insistent call of the mission field. Could these two strong claims on his life be harmoniously reconciled?

"Please let us not part again in silence," he

prayed, longing to put an end to their period of uncertainty.

In this section of the biography, "The Test of Free Time," Elisabeth used Jim's own words and it turned out to be exactly that at intervals, "No work, no money to spend, nothing to do." Jim was afraid of wasting days like these with no prearranged timetable. Without motivation and self-discipline it would have been easy to do so. For a physically vigorous, mentally alert man like Jim, the challenge of too hectic a program would have proved simpler. But he had lived through such a period at college. The present was a complete reversal of the study, socializing, and Christian commitments that he had experienced at Wheaton. Would he weather the storm or go under?

By the end of that same month, on October 29, Jim had taken two positive steps to secure more activity in the future. He felt led to volunteer work for the work among the Quichua Indians in Ecuador, although he waited to post the letter until he had received confirmation from the Lord. This came in his daily Bible reading in Ephesians, the phrase "redeeming the time" striking him as particularly appropriate to his situation. The whole idea was triggered off by reading a letter to Bert from Dr. Wilfred Tidmarsh who was already working there.

He also applied to a local Christian school to work as a substitute teacher. Telling this to Elisabeth in a letter, he mentioned other activities among youngsters in a detention home, and a craft class. He was always willing to lend a hand cheerfully with any project to win the friendship and attention of young people. Knowing Elisabeth's love of literature he kept her informed about his reading list. "I always try to get in what I call 'reprobate reading' . . . just to keep from dropping into the stereotyped and conventional." Then a few days later, "Spent the evening in *The Reader's Digest*, Wordsworth, and Coleridge. Not profitable for sanctifying, but good broadening."

It was hard enough filling his days with rewarding employment without criticism from outsiders. But this is what he encountered, and it rather bothered him although his own conscience was quite clear on the matter. "Why isn't he working?" people were heard to ask without troubling to find out his circumstances.

It didn't make it any easier that he still hadn't finally decided where his sphere of service was likely to be. Letters had arrived from Wilfred Tidmarsh of Ecuador about working with the Quichuas, and also from Rowland Hill of Bangalore who needed a Bible school teacher for well-to-do Hindus, two very dissimilar projects. He spent Christmas apart from Elisabeth and in writing to her afterwards seemed rather satiated with the traditional celebrations.

The start of the New Year and the second half of the twentieth-century made him pause to consider the solemnity of the landmark, "Children born today will see the wind-up of the age," Jim's father had announced. Sometimes it seemed as though Jim lived on an emotional seesaw, encouraged at intervals and then cast down. But with his usual resilience he picked himself up and plunged into whatever job required his attention, taking time to write a letter of encouragement to Elisabeth who was also trying to sort out her problems.

He was never satisfied with his talks to students, but after his death letters came in to his wife telling her of the impact he had on people. "He dared us to give ourselves up to Christ." In a letter to a friend, Jim echoed that expression, "Christ needs some young fellows to sell out to Him and recklessly toss their lives into His work."

Only three days into the New Year, Jim received a letter of acceptance from "Camp Wycliffe" for the summer. This was to be held at the University of Oklahoma and was organized by the Summer Institute of Linguistics. It was to train him for breaking down tribal languages into written symbols and he found himself looking forward to this course of study.

Jim's diary over this period is peppered with quotations from writers whom he found helpful, Amy Carmichael as usual bringing a great deal of solace to him. Many speaking and teaching engagements were noted down, although sometimes the deep winter snowdrifts had prevented him from carrying the earlier ones out.

By mid-April Jim felt sufficiently confident to turn down the offer to finish the year as a teacher at school. He appeared to have peace about this decision because he told Elisabeth, "Though these days may be quiet, as far as doing is concerned, they are jammed full of excitement in the inner man." The waiting time was paying off.

By June 2nd he had traveled to Oklahoma, stopping in at Wheaton on the way. The course lasted ten weeks and it was well-attended by hundreds of students, some of them missionaries who wanted to study unwritten languages. Jim reveled in the intellectual challenge involved in analyzing these unknown tongues. During the course he worked with an informant who had been a missionary to the Quichuas. This man during their time together told Jim about the savage Auca tribe which immediately triggered off a lively interest in Jim's mind. Could this be the area where God wanted him to work? Was it just a straw in the wind or a definite sign from God?

For ten days Jim devoted himself to a special prayer for clear confirmation about his plans. An abandoned mission station among the Quichuas was available for any volunteer, and he wrote, "If it is God's will, I am ready to go immediately." His parents worried whether his outstanding gifts as a teacher and preacher should be used to help American young people rather than a remote and savage tribe. "I dare not stay home while Quichuas perish," he wrote. "The Quichuas must be reached for God." Enough for policy. Now for prayer and practice.

Jim's vision for the spread of the Gospel extended over a larger area even than Ecuador. ". . . The Word must go south into Peru and Bolivia."

# 6

Jim decided to stay on with Bill Cathens after the course was finished, helping in an assembly and working with students on the campus. If there was any encouragement at all, it lay in the fact that a letter had arrived from Dr. Tidmarsh in Ecuador, "I would urge you both to come as soon as possible," he wrote. "All being well, I am planning a leave for myself in the autumn."

Jim pressed on with arrangements for Ecuador, optimistically sending for a passport. At the back of his mind he always hoped that Bill would accompany him there. It felt good to have another young fellow with him in the work, however routine, and they made plans together to cover every aspect. It was quite a tough assignment as they needed to earn their expenses by taking on decorating and repair jobs around the area.

He was already thinking ahead to the supplies they would need to take out with them when a further hint of encouragement reached him. Ed McCully, one of his college mates, had decided to give up school teaching and was contemplating full-time service for the Lord. "Now I wonder if he may not be the man

God would send with us to Ecuador?" Jim even felt the urge to contact Ed personally, ". . . much the same as Barnabas went to Tarsus to seek Saul long ago, needing a companion for his travels."

Acting on this impulse, Jim set off to Wisconsin to probe the situation. While both were engaged in manual jobs to meet their expenses, they managed to fit in three and a half hours of Bible study every other day. Jim's comment, "The interchange of thought is stimulating." However, they decided not to rush into decision-making while they were together, but think over the matter.

A further setback, if it could be so termed, arose when Bill wrote to tell of his forthcoming marriage. That effectively gave the death-blow to Jim's hopes of going out as two single male missionaries together. "Talk of marriage, rings, flowers, weddings, and (ugh!) housekeeping leaves me cold," he wrote to his parents, and when he received a reply from his mother, mildly suggesting that he was probably envious of Bill's happiness, he took some pains to defend his stand on the matter. However, he ended by admitting that ". . . if it becomes clear that one's testimony and effectiveness would be increased, one should marry."

Although anxious to establish churches in the New Testament pattern, founded on Brethren principles, he still became exasperated at times with some of their hairsplitting theology. "The urge comes on me . . . to write in scathing terms for these piddling little magazines of 'comfort and kind words for God's little flock.' " He felt sickened by the overt materialism of some of the Brethren in the Portland area when they should have been involved in reaching out to nonchristians. Jim possessed an uncomfortable and sensitive conscience when it came to sorting out priorities. This prevented him from returning home for Christmas, even though he had been away for seven months. He was always reluctant to indulge himself even in simple family pleasures if he felt duty called him in the other direction, although each member remained very dear to him.

The beginning of another year, 1951, found Jim working in even closer harmony with Ed McCully. That urge to contact him a few months previously had proved an inspired move. They tackled any Christian assignment that arose for the next six months and paid their way by working on a series of casual jobs. Touches of poetic description illuminate the pages of his journal. A description of a walk on a spring evening makes him burst out in involuntary worship, "Oh the fullness, pleasure, sheer excitement of knowing God on earth."

Setting up a radio program with Ed presented a new challenge. They took turns preaching and announcing for each other. In between speaking engagements they tried to earn a little money by selling, but the funds were slow coming in. Fortunately Jim's sense of humor usually surfaced and burst out irrepressibly in his journal comments: "We figured we had plenty of 'religion' for that day, so went off to Zarrit's for coffee, and contact with the high school kids." He enjoyed clowning with Ed in unrehearsed incidents. It was this balance in his nature which made him a "whole" man, not a religious fanatic, and so endeared him to others; preacher and poet, wrestler and prayer-warrior, disciple and decorator, Bible scholar and garbage collector.

Not all the speaking engagements were rewarding. He was glad to be asked into a local prison to preach to the inmates of the forgiveness which only God can give, but rather downhearted with some of his efforts in the high school. "Six weeks so far, and no natives converted except that salesman who was out of town. We feel God must be testing us . . ."

In spite of cramped living conditions and lack of ready cash, they evolved a harmonious program together, cooking for each other in the evening when they returned home exhausted. Afterwards they shared a common love of poetry—an empathy appeared to be springing up between them which would become an important factor later on when they operated in a larger team.

On the whole there were few results from their ministry at this stage. Jim found his stimulation in reading not only the Bible but missionary biographies such as C. T. Studd's, "that gaunt, bearded giant with the fiery words and ringing laugh." He felt moved to pray for missionary friends around the world. By the summer he was also moved to comment, "Looking back over the last two years since graduation gives me a funny sense of uselessness . . . but I have sought the will of God—our orders are to obey . . . Who shall doubt or say that our labors are in vain?"

Jim attended Ed's and Bill's weddings that summer and then enjoyed the novelty of his first plane ride. "Thrilled at the wonders of the air." His exact resources upon arriving home were $1.20 so he started immediately earning money with manual jobs. However, at last things seemed on the move. He had met the Tidmarsh family for ten days. Talking with them had reaffirmed his plans for Ecuador. He had applied for a visa and been given permission by the military authorities to leave the States. With Ed and his new wife Marilou at medical school in Los Angeles, Jim began to pray for a single fellow to join him in Ecuador, wondering if Pete Fleming from the University of Washington might prove the answer.

"I would certainly be glad if God persuaded you to go with me," Jim wrote to Pete. "But HE must persuade you . . . All I can do is pray for a cleared path for you." Jim must have wished for a cleared path also in his arrangements with Elisabeth. They met again at her home after quite a long absence. Neither had any doubt about their love for each other but no clear certainty about marriage.

In the next month, October, they snatched another few days together. "Dinner at the hotel in Littleton . . . she wore pearl earrings for me . . . she sat at my feet while Pete read." But when she wept a little as she said goodbye, she could not have known that this would be the last time they met before Jim sailed in 1952. One thing had been established, that Elisabeth should eventually go to Ecuador as enquiries in other areas had come to nothing. Jim felt overwhelmed with his many blessings. There were no hard feelings or recriminations against the Lord for the many frustrations he had endured over the past two years. "I am particularly conscious of the Christian's right to expect events to be exactly timed for good. 'As for God, His way is perfect.' "

It seemed at last as though things were really coming together. In spite of two years' hard slog, often dull and unrewarding at times, Jim had shown he was capable of taking on a demanding, routine schedule. He wasn't just a highly academic product of Bible college who couldn't relate his head knowledge to the needs of the world outside. He had also proved he wasn't daunted by sheer, hard physical work nor afraid of existing with very little money in his pocket. Beyond doubt, he had established that he had been called to serve God in Ecuador and had made contact with the Tidmarsh family. Even his request for a visa was already in the mail. His love for Elisabeth had grown and the way was now open for her to travel to Ecuador also. They had stood the test of separation from each other so far. Who but Elisabeth would have been willing to love Jim with no definite outcome for some time to the relationship?

Then, too, his knowledge of God had deepened and matured. By faithfully recording his spiritual peaks and troughs he had given future readers an intimate glimpse of his soul's progress, but he never lost hope through the setbacks and discouragements. God had revealed himself to be more than equal to any situation.

Finally, in Ed he had secured a valuable and reliable team member for the enterprise ahead with the possibility of being joined by Pete also. His body was toughened and strengthened by the physical chores he had undertaken and he hadn't lost his sense of humor—a most necessary asset for any servant of the Lord. Flashes of the former high-spirited student burst out when a celebration to relieve tension was called for.

He had resisted the temptation to join his brother Bert (which many of the Brethren had expected him to do) and remained steadfast in his determination to take the Gospel to an unreached tribe although his parents would have been delighted to see him serving the Lord in the United States of America. It was hard to remain singleminded when the needs of his own country remained so evident, and family pressure, though subtle and well-meant, was put upon him. Jim had a good relationship with both his parents so it couldn't have been easy to resist their pleas.

After meetings in New York which he had shared with Pete Fleming, the two young men drove back together to Portland. Little time remained to him there but he still managed to fulfill several speaking engagements. As usual his quiet times proved a source of challenge and encouragement, yet also a safety valve to express the doubts and disappointments which cropped up even though he was confident he was following God's blueprint for his life.

Assembling supplies for Ecuador took top priority. Nearly forty years ago, when Jim was planning his itinerary, transport still wasn't as readily available as today. Mission Aviation planes performed a marvelous job in flying in to inaccessible areas but they were few and far between. Basically he realized he would need to take in most of his personal necessities for his first term of service, apart from food. There were times too when he would have to rely completely on native supplies.

On a trip upriver in November 1952, for instance, he took his own lunch with him, "lemons and sugar for lemonade, a few pieces of buriju (a jungle partridge we bought yesterday), a bit of chocolate and cheese, and a hardboiled egg apiece." Later, however, the Indians brought their own delicacies as a gift, "milky chica . . . a tender bit of tapir shoulder (the best meat I've had while here), manioc and steamed green bananas." Two months previously he made an entry in his journal about a rare delicacy, "Ate my first ants yesterday—toasted 'ukui'."

Of course some of the sophisticated recording equipment on sale today for language students was not on the market when Jim was collecting his priorities. Nor did he possess a great deal of money for anything but essentials and he was naturally limited by the weight of containers which had to be transported.

A Bible Society report on Ecuador in 1987 claims that, "Despite its oil, Ecuador is still one of the least developed countries in South America." In Jim Elliot's time oil was beginning to be developed as a natural resource and some national income was derived from coffee and banana plantations but on no large scale. It is now, and has been for many years, a land of tremendous contrasts with a wealthy minority and a very poor majority.

Physical features of the country include high mountain ranges, coastal plains and some areas of dense jungle. The people themselves are derived from many races and speak a large number of languages, but the most dominant group is that of the Quichua people.

The Bible Society comments that "It is encouraging to see many of the Quichua people turning to God. Only ten years ago virtually none of these people were Christians, but today over 150,000 are believers." It was a very different picture when Jim Elliot was getting ready to travel there as a missionary. Intermittent work had gone on for a number of years in that country, but the problems of slow communications and many different languages ensured only little progress in spite of dedicated Christians.

A situation like this posed a tremendous challenge. It certainly wasn't going to be a walk-over and gain easy glory for anyone. Jim was prepared—even enthusiastic—to take on the assignment. Back in his college days in 1949 he had written, "He is no fool who gives what he cannot keep to gain what he cannot lose," not knowing then what the future would hold for him. When his brother Bert was leaving home for the mission field, Jim wrote to his parents, "Our silken selves must know denial."

# 7

The first day of the New Year brought a triumphant entry in the journal. "This is the first of these miracles I am encouraged to expect." This miracle was none other than the total amount of Jim's fare to Guayaquil coming in from five different sources in twenty-four hours, the donors all being people Jim had met during the past few months. This came as encouraging confirmation to him.

The usual last-minute preparations had to be fitted in among speaking engagements and bidding farewell to friends and relatives. Injections were another necessity, sorting out mail, and loading everything on board the *Santa Juana* on time. Then after all the frantic rush, Jim found himself with three extra days to spare when the ship was late arriving. He filled in the time with more letter-writing. February 4th found him writing, "The *Santa Juana* is on the way . . . now I am actually at sea—as a passenger, of course, but at sea nevertheless, and bound for Ecuador . . . Joy, sheer joy, and thanksgiving fill and encompass me . . . I can do nothing but sing out Hallelujah!"

At the same time, he almost felt guilty that he

experienced no feelings of sadness as his parents waved him goodbye at the quayside. They shed a few tears but Jim was filled with a sense of exultation. All he had worked for, all he had dreamed about was at last coming to pass. There could well have been doubts and reservations at the back of his mind because Jim was setting out with no guaranteed financial support, but happily these considerations carried no weight with him. Everything had "worked together for good" in the end, even the extra four days delay had given more time for preparation.

Pete Fleming shared a cabin with Jim and they were thankful no other passenger turned up to occupy the third empty bunk. Jim wrote reassuring letters home to his parents about conditions on board, spiced with touches of humor. His descriptive powers were called upon to do justice to some of the strange birds and sea-creatures he noticed on the voyage. Jim's zest for living and great happiness at that stage shine through his writing, "The sheer joy of being in the will of God and the knowledge of His direction is my general experience now." It would have been easy for Jim in youthful impatience to have "jumped the gun" and gone ahead of the Lord's guidance two years previously, but though the delay had seemed tedious at times, in retrospect he could see the benefits of waiting for the "all clear" at each stage.

Jim and Peter enjoyed all the new sights and soon were on good terms with both passengers and crew. They took no pains to conceal the fact that they were going out as missionaries and had some interesting discussions with various ship's officers and they were able to practice their halting Spanish on several occasions. On the sixth day out there was an unexpected stop at Manzanillo, Mexico, to off-load a sick crew member. Pete and Jim spent a good few hours chatting with Spanish-speaking cabdrivers in the town plaza.

Another evening was passed with stevedores by the holds while they were shifting cargo and they also picked up many useful facts about the new country for which they were bound. Jim commented that the first week at sea had "passed terribly fast" for them although some of the passengers were already complaining of the boredom. "Thank God for purpose in life," he wrote. The two friends were determined to make use of every opportunity for witnessing, practicing Spanish, increasing their knowledge of Ecuador or simply for enjoying the novelty of their first seavoyage.

Making the most of their new experience, they seized the chance to go ashore after ten days. Anchoring off San Salvador, they were ferried to land with other passengers and then hired a car to the capital.

Twelve days out from home they landed in the Canal Zone and enjoyed some fellowship with Brethren in that area. Jim found the whole experience an eye-opener, and felt impelled to pass on the information about the many opportunities there to the folks at home. "It makes me responsible, terribly so!" Would anyone be stirred to start a work there?

Jim and Peter had also been invited to join the captain and steward on a fishing expedition on a high-powered launch which provided them with a fascinating chance of sport and also an opportunity to witness. All these novel experiences afforded valuable material to be written up in letters home to Elisabeth and to his parents. Jim was always eager to share his exploits with his family. His letters and journals don't come across as merely "preachy" or written with one eye to posterity, but a vivid medley of sounds, sights and impressions with an occasional involuntary and very natural spiritual comment flowing spontaneously from the heart. "Hurry the promise, Lord, that 'the earth shall be filled with the glory of the Lord.' Lord, open his heart to the Lord Jesus. Lord, send laborers! God be praised for an understanding older worker."—all random phrases picked from the pages of his journal written on the sea voyage.

All too soon the first part of the voyage on the *Santa Juana* was over. For seventeen days, Jim had reveled in his life on board, absorbing everything that was unique and different. Perhaps from his family's earlier years in Seattle he had inherited a love for the sea. He admitted at the start, "I wanted to sail when I was in grammar school." The next boat, *Santa Rosita*, a small yacht, came alongside the larger vessel to take off passengers and cargo, depositing them at Guayaquil after a sea trip of four hours. Dr. Tidmarsh failed to greet them on the quayside, owing to an incorrect message being relayed to Quito, but they caught up with him the next day. One unexpected bonus befell them in that customs officials levied no duty at all on their combined luggage, which amazed them but at the same time filled their hearts with gratitude to a great God who cared for them in every detail.

With eagerness Jim gazed out of the plane windows on his first flight over Ecuador to pick out distinguishing features of the landscape, ". . . we saw the great quilt of the plateau, beautiful and quiet with terraced hillsides and occasional buildings." Waiting on the tarmac was Gwen Tidmarsh and her son Rob to welcome them and take them for temporary accommodation at their home. The first evening was spent chatting about their future work, particularly the news that it might be possible to buy a small outpost to be as near as possible to the Auca tribe.

Exciting as this project seemed, Jim and Peter were immediately confronted with a much harder one, that of learning Spanish, but it had to be mastered before either fellow could make much impact on the natives. An occasional note of frustration can be detected in Jim's comments in his journal. How he longed to master the language quickly so he could make good, personal contacts! As ever, though, his artistic eye was attracted to the different aspects of his new surroundings and a vivid word picture described the city and the marketplace in a letter to his parents.

In a few days, he left the comparative sophistication of city life for a much more primitive existence. Gradually he was being acclimatized to what he could expect when he worked with the Aucas. After spending his first night under mosquito netting, he took a long and tortuous trip in a pickup truck to stay with the Shorts in Santo Domingo. They were the only missionaries in the area and, as usual, Jim made himself useful in "the little things." He had learned to do just this through the discipline of the last two years, "washing dishes, helping with the kids . . . driving the truck." He never questioned this, however, but cheerfully accepted whatever chores came his way. Accompanying him on the expedition was a young Ecuadorian called Abdon who was studying English and in turn could help Jim with his Spanish.

He could not have found a more compatible companion than Pete in his first missionary enterprise. Like Jim, Pete led a thoroughly balanced life at college with honors in basketball and golf. Studying philosophy at Washington University, he received his master's degree in 1951. Initially, he experienced some problems in reconciling Christian thought with philosophical ideals, which was perhaps only to be expected, but after an inward struggle, the Word of God won the battle of his mind.

Peter had been converted at the age of thirteen by a blind evangelist and during his college years his fellow students were impressed by his consistent Christian testimony. Many were surprised when, after corresponding with Jim, he spread the news that God had called him to work in Ecuador, but to him it was only a natural step in obedience. Another matter which brought him close to Jim was in affairs of the heart. Pete was engaged to Olive Ainslie whom he had known since childhood, but he, too, saw no immediate prospect of marriage. Writing to Dr. Tidmarsh prior to leaving he stated, " 'He that taketh not up his cross, and followeth after Me is not worthy of Me' . . . it has seemed that the severe requirements of a difficult field like Ecuador are matched on a spiritual level by the severe requirements placed on real disciples."

Another significant quote from the same letter stated, " 'He that findeth his life shall lose it: and he that loseth his life for My sake shall find it' (Matt. 10:39)." It might be easy to copy a portion of Scripture down in his first enthusiasm to become a missionary, but when the real challenge came, Pete was more than ready to meet it head on.

To Jim, waiting to greet Betty in Ecuador, Pete fulfilled a very necessary role as a like-minded confidant who could enter into his own emotional problems. How Jim longed to see Betty again and yet he had no concrete proposal to offer her about their future together. "Betty should be in Ecuador a week from today," he confided in his journal, counting the hours.

If anyone thought their relationship appeared cold and unnatural, how little they really knew of Jim and Elisabeth. It may have been five years since they first met with still no apparent progress in their mutual affairs, but their love for one another was growing deeper and it was becoming increasingly difficult to make no specific decisions about their joint future. In her book *Passion and Purity*, Elisabeth revealed her first impression of Jim as a student. "Met Jim Elliot. Good talk. Wonderful guy. The more Jim talked, the more I saw that he fit the picture of what I hoped for in a husband. As for Jim, he had said, 'I'm hungry for you Bett, but you're not mine.' "

And it was Elisabeth who chose a quotation from C. S. Lewis at the start of her book. "The only place outside heaven where you can be perfectly safe from all the dangers and perturbations of love is hell." She well knew the frustrations, not of unrequited love but of unconsummated love with no firm promises to which she could cling. She would rather retain her tenuous link with Jim in spite of all the anxieties and uncertainties than be released and search for material security, and lose contact with the man she loved.

Then in April Betty at last arrived. Jim enjoyed showing her the old mud-walled town with its exotic sights and scenes. With a group of friends they attended their first bullfight on Labor Day. Jim waxed lyrical on the graceful movements and skill of the matadors yet remained strangely unmoved by the suffering of the animals.

For the next few months until mid-August they reveled in each other's company, alone and with friends. Sometimes Jim feared he had upset her by his clumsiness and inability to set a wedding date. Mostly he found Elisabeth sweet and understanding but occasionally she felt a little wounded by circumstances. They set off for several marathon hikes among the breathtaking mountain scenery which called for all Jim's descriptive powers when he entrusted the account to the pages of his journal. Together they studied Spanish—Jim moved into a Spanish doctor's house to gain the benefit of speaking the language all the time. It was also necessary to gain some basic knowledge of elementary medicine and tropical diseases from Dr. Tidmarsh for later on when they would be based far from civilization.

On the whole, it proved a particularly happy time for the two lovers, notwithstanding the debit and credit balance. "I have not lost one nameable thing by putting her and our whole relationship in the simplest way possible into His hands," declared Jim in

May. By July he was writing, "I wonder sometimes if it is right to be so happy. Day follows day in an easy succession of wonders and joys—simple good things like food well-prepared, or play with children, or conversation with Peter, or supply of money for rent or board within hours of its being due." Truly, Jim's "cup was running over."

# 8

*P*ete, too, felt overwhelmed by God's goodness at that crucial period. "These almost six months have been crammed full of goodness ... and undoubtedly we have learned things which will stand us in good stead all our missionary lives ... it has been a terrific boon praying together and seeing God give us faith." Earlier he had written, "I am longing now to reach the Aucas ... I would gladly give my life for that tribe."

Years previously at Wheaton, Jim had stated, "One does not surrender a life in an instant. That which is lifelong can only be surrendered in a lifetime." So the two friends were both of the same mind and persuasion not just for an emotional moment but through convictions they had held for years.

An unexpected thrill occurred when Jim was offered a quick trip to the eastern jungle from where he could fly over Auca territory. Great stuff! At last he was getting within sight of his objective. The fact that they didn't spot any Auca houses didn't dampen his enthusiasm. "They may be only a few hundred in number, but they are part of the whole creation, and we have orders for such."

Jim made rapid strides in picking up Spanish, in spite of his fears. After five months he was given his first opportunity to preach in that language and although he wasn't completely satisfied with his performance, he enjoyed the experience and gained confidence from it. By August, the two fellows were scheduled to move on again, this time to Shandia; thus ending what Jim regarded as "five of the happiest months of my life." Although anxious to meet the Auca situation, he hated saying farewell to Elisabeth without being able to promise her a definite time for their engagement. He confessed to her afterwards, in a letter, that he had paced under her windows in the early morning darkness, reluctant to put a distance between the two of them.

It had been a precious time for Elisabeth, too, the longest they'd ever spent together. Previously their short visits to each other's families had taken place in the sophisticated civilization of North America. Even their parents' modest homes achieved an acceptable standard of comfort but life in Quito had proved much more down-to-earth, a sort of halfway house between Portland and Shandia. In *Strange Ashes* Elisabeth looked back wistfully on those months together. "Jim and I walked in the pastures on the outskirts of town, had climbed Pichincha, and seen the sun rise as the moon was setting over the city . . . had explored the byways of the old sections of the town, practicing our Spanish on friendly shopkeepers and children." Yet Jim was bound for work among the Quichua Indians, and Elisabeth had to reconcile herself to little or no news of him while she spent several months in language work on the other side of the Andes.

Squeezing on to an already crowded bus, the two men enjoyed the novel journey and all the unfamiliar sights as the vehicle crept slowly up the steep mountain slopes. The descent on the other side was equally breathtaking with views of tributaries of the Amazon spreading out over the level areas. By the time they reached Shell Mera, which had once been an oil prospecting town, Jim and Peter were glad to climb down and stretch their lanky legs which had been cramped after hours of traveling. It didn't take long to stride around the few old remaining buildings. At the Missionary Aviation Fellowship base they met Dr. Tidmarsh again. During the last decade, the Mission's valiant little planes had revolutionized missionary travel, taking a couple of hours to reach areas which had previously required days of footslogging on the trail.

Facilities for flights remained minimal at that stage. Shandia, the outlying station, possessed no airstrip so when the missionaries needed to reach there, they were dropped as near as possible and then had to set out on a three-hour trek through virgin jungle. After stumbling and fighting their way in a race against the sudden oncoming of darkness, they could have been excused for feeling less than enthusiastic about their new surroundings. But the reverse was true. "My joy is full," wrote Jim, "right on time . . . God's time." Suddenly all the years of waiting and preparation made sense. Around the small clearing hacked out for the town, tall trees stretched up into the sky, their tops vying with each other for a glimpse of the hot tropical sun. Lush creepers intertwined their trunks; exotic butterflies fluttered in the open space. Dangerous snakes lay coiled in the dense undergrowth. Incredibly beautiful orchids displayed their muted colors while fungi of every description dazzled the eye of the onlooker with their brilliant hues.

All this the two young men noted in their first forest trek. And at the other end they were thrilled to meet Quichua Indian families—so many new impressions in a few short hours! All these flora and fauna and the men and women waiting to greet them were familiar to Dr. Tidmarsh, who accompanied them. He had lived in this environment for several years and was only leaving reluctantly to seek medical help for his wife who had been injured in an accident.

He led the way to his thatched house made of split bamboo and erected on stilts to give more air round the building, and protect it from the many thousands of insects which swarmed on the damp ground. Pete and Jim gazed around with keen interest and liked what they saw. It would provide more than ample shelter for them in the months that lay ahead. One immediate problem faced them though. Having just become conversant with Spanish after their crash courses, they now had to come to grips with Quichua before they could communicate with the very people to whom they had longed to pass on the Gospel. Would they be able to surmount this fresh obstacle? ". . . I know all the same that I must get it—get it good and get it rapidly," wrote Jim. "By Thy grace, good Lord, I'm going to."

Yet the main difficulty was not their application or desire but the sheer impossibility of achieving any consecutive hours of study time during the day. So many interruptions crowded in as the Indians with their *laissez-faire* outlook on life had no conception of the need for concentrated periods of work, and came to Jim and Pete selling food, asking for advice on the work of clearing a new airstrip and demanding pay for their services at the most inconvenient moments.

Jim, too, was a little concerned about the house in which they were living. It fell abysmally short of Western standards of any acceptable norm but ". . . it keeps the Indians' level of living too far below ours to get really next to them in the psychological sense." The screened windows in their bedroom looked out over the river and the airstrip. A curtain separated that room from the living quarters where they even boasted a couple of rugs and two aluminum chairs. The debris of mud and dead insects was swept out daily by an Indian.

They adapted reasonably well to the diet which consisted mainly of fruit, with the occasional addition of meat after an Indian hunting expedition. To supplement, they took doses of vitamin pills and also started a small garden for an extra crop of vegetables. "They don't know anything about these vegetables here," wrote Jim as he went to meet the plane which flew in supplies of celery, onions, tomatoes and cucumbers. Occasionally they were treated to a meal of fish when the Indians had been successful by the banks of the river. It all helped to vary the monotony about which Pete and Jim never complained. They were game to eat almost anything, even roasted ants.

Both were fascinated by the Quichuas now that they were in a position to observe them more closely. This interest was reciprocated by the Indians who just couldn't get over the fact of how much writing the white men did. They were always covering reams of paper. Pete and Jim were delighted when the Indians complimented them on speaking Quichua so fluently. As their confidence grew, Dr. Tidmarsh took them along when he was called out on errands of healing. They didn't tackle anything too complicated, possessing neither the equipment nor the expertise to do so. Often it was childbirth which took place in primitive squalor with no hygienic, modern refinements. It was no use grieving overmuch when they lost a new baby. The Indians certainly didn't; human life was held cheaply by them.

Bedtime came at nine-thirty and they rose at five-thirty, taking advantage of as many daylight hours as possible. Jim experimented with growing crops by different methods. The multifarious insects had taken a heavy toll of the first tender seedlings. Most of the men's energies were directed toward helping with the school and overseeing the labor on the airstrip. By the last day in September Jim could write triumphantly to Betty, "Radio contacts all morning covering the first flight to Shandia. Easily a hundred and fifty Indians gathered for the event . . . Praised God for success and rapidity in getting the strip done."

Jim still hankered after a quicker grasp of the language. " . . . we need the language to get over the first great hurdle of missionary jungle life. Then the war really begins in earnest, and we are eager for it." He thoroughly enjoyed his involvement with the pupils at the four-grade school, not only with lessons but in teaching them games and a team spirit which was completely foreign to their concepts and way of life. Slide shows, which were restricted by the amount of electricity available, and concerns over the radio both served to widen the boys' horizons and improve Jim's and Pete's vocabulary.

Jim also earned the Indians' respect by taking part in their games. Although he had tried to teach them volleyball, which wasn't particularly successful at first because the Indian boys had no idea of playing as a team, Jim had no intention of imposing his American culture on theirs. He was equally willing to learn from them and encourage their skills also. The influence of his early "renaissance" experience stayed with him for the rest of his life and made him oblivious to criticism if he felt sincerely that what he was doing was right before the Lord.

The Indians needed all the small diversions they could arrange as their lives contained plenty of deprivation and sorrow. Death was always just around the corner either from childbirth, infant mortality, snake bites or tropical diseases. They led a precarious existence with very few comforts, particularly by Western standards. Jim and Pete longed to be able to share the Gospel with them to give them some hope for the future.

Both his parents and Elisabeth received long letters with vivid descriptions of the beauty of the tropical valley and the foothills of the Andes. They were left in no doubt about the different kinds of foods he ate, and the work in which he was involved constructing a clinic and widening the airstrip. To Betty he confided, "I do fear sometimes, like a worrying mother, that something will happen to you and I will lose you; then what would I do? . . ." But it was only in his journal he wrote of his frustrations and impatience because progress in everything was so slow. "O God, life is slow, for all the action it holds." Would nothing ever reach fruition?

Another couple of people were also chafing at their lack of progress. Ed McCully, Jim's friend from college days, and his wife Marilou, together with young Stevie, arrived in Quito in December 1952, to start Spanish language studies and to move to Shandia as soon as they had mastered the essentials. Ed had already worked with Jim in Chester where he had more than proved his worth. After marriage, he had enrolled for a year at the School of Missionary Medicine in Los Angeles to learn the basics of tropical diseases and other health care he would require when he actually reached a field station. It looked as though the strands of the enterprise were slowly being drawn together with three young men firmly committed to carrying the Gospel to the Aucas. But they were to be confronted with a very severe test to their faith in the not too distant future.

The new year of 1953, however, started with one heartwarming incident. Elisabeth was intrigued and excited to be handed a telegram by a friend on horseback late one night. "Meet me in Quito," read the message from Jim. After two-days grueling travel the two met up together. "I gave Betty an engagement ring last night in front of the fireplace," Jim wrote to his parents afterwards. It was no rushed decision. "I think I have the will of God in this." He would have given it to her earlier but had not wanted to leave Peter on his own in Shandia and so had to wait until Dr. Tidmarsh was going there.

Even then Jim warned Betty it could be yet another five years before they were free to marry. "I have promised to put up some buildings for other missionaries first. Also I want you to learn Quichua before we are married."

Elisabeth accepted all the conditions, with mental reservations about another long wait. But she loved Jim and if that was the way he wanted it, she would comply with his wishes.

# 9

The first challenge to their happiness came after just one week. On a routine chest X-ray, Elisabeth was diagnosed as having tuberculosis. She immediately felt this would prove a death knell to all their plans for the future. Even if cured, life in a tropical jungle would never be suitable for her again.

Jim had no such reservations. "If God has allowed us to become engaged, He can cope with this crisis." In the end his faith was rewarded, and Elisabeth was given a clean bill of health by the next week's check. It must have seemed a long, anxious seven days for her. They would never know whether God had miraculously healed her or merely decided to test their faith by this apparent mistake.

Ed arrived by plane for a preliminary visit to make plans for building a house just as Pete went down with a severe attack of malaria, so Jim was particularly glad of his company. After Ed's departure, the two fellows struggled on with building in rainy weather, and trying to grasp more of the language in their spare moments. A precious interlude was a fortnight spent in Quito at a conference and then shopping with Elisabeth for necessities in Shandia.

Traveling in that area always remained an unpredictable hazard. Apart from mechanical failures, the state of the roads made transport a risky procedure, especially in a rainy season such as the one that was just commencing. In addition to delays of the usual nature, Jim was further frustrated by the loss of his bag with all its contents on the trip, probably thrown off with other luggage before he reached his destination. "The Lord gave me a victory in the loss," wrote Jim to Betty, "reminding me to be thankful for the abundance of possessions I have had." Yet when Elisabeth received the letter, she read between the lines, seeing his weariness and depression there. It wasn't so much losing his clothes, camera and harmonica, but the box containing a selection of the best slides he had ever taken. These were irreplaceable and naturally Elisabeth shared his dejection.

Her immediate work on the Colarado tongue had come to an end and she was confident that her language files and notebook, acquired over a year of much painful, personal experience would be of value to someone taking over translation work in the future. Now she turned her attention to the next pressing matter, which was to gain a working knowledge of the Quichua language in as short a time as possible. Unashamedly, she acknowledged to herself that this language study was more urgent than either Spanish or Colarado because as soon as she became conversant in it, she would at last be free to marry Jim.

Elisabeth moved to stay with a missionary family in the eastern jungle. Carol Conn, her hostess, was already fluent in Quichua and Elisabeth learned avidly from her, from talking to Indians around the house, and attending church services and Bible studies. This was no formal tuition with notebooks and an accredited teacher but an on-the-spot immediate immersion into everyday, conversational Quichua, and the method began to work quickly. Soon Elisabeth found her industry was paying off and she was beginning to communicate, albeit falteringly.

A second heavy blow fell just about that time. Elisabeth received a letter from her colleague, Doreen, announcing that all her Colarado language materials had been stolen. Again the tragedy happened when her suitcase disappeared from the top of a bus, an occupational hazard in that part of the world. She tried to believe that the box, notebook and charts would turn up again eventually. It couldn't be duplicated because it only existed in a single copy of her own handwriting, but her prayers were never realized.

While she was still hoping against hope, the most savage blow of all fell. On a routine daily radio contact with all the mission stations connected to the Missionary Aviation Fellowship, Elisabeth heard Jim's voice coming over, tense and urgent. "The brink of the cliff is only five yards from the house now. The river is eating away the base of the cliff . . ." The silence that followed over the next two days could only mean one thing. Shandia was no more. The three old buildings he had repaired and the two new ones he had constructed had disappeared into the turbulent, swirling river waters.

In one sense, it didn't come completely as a surprise to Betty. Jim had warned her in letters, that according to the Indians, this rainy season was the worst in thirty years. But no one had visualized that the whole of Jim and Peter's first year's work would be completely destroyed. Most of the chattels had been salvaged and were distributed in various dumps on safer ground away from the river. Even a portion of the new airstrip was washed away. Elisabeth coaxed a party of Indians to accompany her to Shandia to offer whatever help they could and when they arrived Jim filled in the details for her. He had barely escaped with his life when a sudden cliff fall nearly precipitated him into the angry, swollen river.

"Weekend was a weary one, brightened only by Betty's coming here on Sunday," Jim wrote in his journal. Then came the depressing task of salvaging usable material and discarding the losses. Small wonder that Jim was struck down with his first bout of malaria at this stage. Apart from the physical symptoms of dizziness, fever, a blinding headache and a raging thirst, his thoughts were thoroughly disoriented and he could not control the distressing mental images. It took him several days to make even a partial recovery.

Urgent decisions needed to be made. Was God indicating through the destruction of Shandia that they had chosen the wrong center for their missionary enterprise? As soon as Jim felt sufficiently strong, he set out with Pete and Ed to survey the whole area. For three weeks they alternately struggled on foot through the dense, tropical jungle or paddled canoes down the Bobinaza River to weigh up the pros and cons of various possible settlements. Betty was left behind with the flimsy protection of a tent in Shandia to guard the valuable equipment that remained.

Footsore and with aching muscles they finally returned. Far from feeling dejected about their physical condition, however, they were full of confidence that they had arrived at a sensible conclusion. Shandia was to be redeveloped as the main base, but in addition, they would build several smaller out-stations. This was the only way in which they could effectively reach the scattered groups of Indians who were spread thinly over a wide area.

The most thrilling news was of an invitation to live in Puyupungu and set up a school there. This came from an Indian man, Atanasio, who had fifteen children. Uncharacteristically of Indians, he had welcomed them and urged them to settle. "Because of God, will you not stay?" he asked them. Who could resist such a plea? The McCullys were deemed the most suitable to stay in Shandia as they wished to begin a study of the Quichua language. Pete was chosen to support them in this project but a couple were needed to open up the new work. Who could take on that task?

At this stage Jim asked Betty, "How soon will you marry me?" with complete assurance that God's perfect timing had arrived at last. All doubts had disappeared. This was the assignment that He had chosen for them to tackle together. If their courtship had appeared unconventional, how much more their marriage arrangements! Fortunately, both partners were of the same mind that the customary elaborate wedding ceremony with expensive trimmings was not for them. "There is something in me that resists the showy part of weddings with a passion I have against few other things in life," wrote Jim. This was no indication of a matter-of-fact relationship. For months, even years, Jim had been confiding in his diary of his longing for Elisabeth, "I have given myself over to the love of her. Oh how I long for her—all of her, her help and counsel and just her presence here, but most of all . . . for her body."

Jim was prepared for criticism and misunderstandings about their arrangements. In a letter to his father, advising him of their intention to marry on October 8, 1953, he admitted, "Few have tried to understand our long waiting for engagement and my going to the jungle single. Few really thought we were the perfect match in the first place."

The civil ceremony took all of ten minutes to perform in the Quito Registry Office with Dr. and Mrs. Tidmarsh as the official witnesses and the McCullys there as friends and partners in the work. The honeymoon was spent in Panama and Costa Rica and then they had to return to Quito to pack their few belongings before they moved on to set up their new quarters. They had managed to contact Jim's brother Dave in Costa Rica. "There we gaped and gawked at the store windows like a couple of palm-leaf savages!" Yet their actual needs were few as little of the stuff Jim had originally brought from the States had been used up to that time. So unpacking their missionary barrels proved quite exciting, with fresh discoveries of forgotten possessions.

With all their drums and crates they flew to Shell Mera and stayed the night with Nate Saint, the Missionary Aviation pilot, and his wife Marj. God was drawing together the team for Operation Auca, although not all of the members were yet aware of their involvement at that stage. Pete and Ed had already joined Jim and now Nate was offering valuable assistance. One by one the wives would supply a valuable back-up service as they stood by their husbands in the arena.

Elisabeth and Jim made a dramatic entry to their new village, arriving on canoes stacked high with their gear. Other crafts carrying Atanasio and his friends gave them a hearty welcome on the river but his womenfolk and children watched their arrival from afar, hiding behind trees.

Elisabeth soon had to come to grips with missionary life in the raw again when they were forced to abandon their thatched house for a large tent because it was overrun with cockroaches and constructed with low beams which allowed neither of them to stand upright. Her previous year in Ecuador with all its disappointments and frustrations had already prepared her to a certain extent, but now new situations and fresh challenges would present themselves.

Within days Jim fell victim to a mysterious fever which laid him on his back for three weeks. Elisabeth anxiously cranked the radio set to communicate with the doctor as none of the usual drugs had any effect. The tent hardly provided an ideal sickroom with water pouring under the sides, but it eventually provided their only shelter for five months. In spite of difficulties, however, Jim made an entry in his journal in early December, "Married life is rich . . . we have known nothing but harmony."

Fortunately, Jim was sufficiently recovered later in the month for them to walk a nine-hour trail, with a young Indian boy as guide, through dense jungle territory to be met at Puyo by Marj Saint. She whisked them off to Shell Mera from where they flew to Shandia for Christmas.

Their ever-threatening enemy, excessive rain, began to trouble them from the start as Jim struggled "with a few helpers to build his own house and also create an airstrip where Nate Saint could land with supplies. Entries in Jim's journal appeared far less frequent once he could confide in Elisabeth and talk matters over with her. A single entry in December imparted some typical information, "It is not raining . . . but the fresh-cut bamboo slats are chunked with fresh mud, the other half of the tent, not yet floored, is slippery gum from an all-night rain on Sunday."

Betty, however, "all woman" as Jim referred to her, was undeterred by her unpromising surroundings and thought it not at all incongruous to cover a card table with a flowery cloth and decorate it with a candle and a forest plant. And while he lay convalescing, Jim, also, had been able to abstract himself from the sea of mud around him by reading a selection of books including *Wuthering Heights* and C. S. Lewis's *Miracles*. But— joy of joys—"Bett and I are reading Amy Carmichael's biography together . . . it stirs me, kept me awake even." Both of them could identify with Amy's many frustrations and obstacles in her missionary pathway as well as rejoice in her triumphs and periods of spiritual uplifting and closeness to the Lord. It must have been a healing therapy to forget the quagmire which surrounded them and be transported in mind to enjoy mental closeness to such a kindred spirit.

The beginning of February brought a ray of hope. "Finished the roof of the house and outhouse today." Yet, a cautionary note, "Men wearying some and dropping off work. Only the Lord is constant and sure." Jim confessed to moments of irritation with some of the workmen, quite understandable in the trying circumstances, yet he blamed himself for his impatience and tried to put the matter right immediately.

It must have been with a profound sense of relief that on April 1st Jim penned the words, "Pause late on a rainy afternoon. Gratefully settled in our home . . . for a week now . . . God has been faithful, though Satan has fought us to discouragement through long weeks of rain."

# 10

The Lord of the elements had not seen fit to spare his servants the drudgery of battling against the weather for several months. Even after moving into the house, the airstrip was still not quite complete. However, other compensations lay in store. Jim's father arrived by the middle of the next month. Far from coming for a holiday, he was soon busily engaged in helping with the construction of a more permanent house in Shandia. Puyupungu would fulfil its intended role as an out-station. Another joy for Jim was his time spent with Ed McCully, both working in the forest and exchanging ideas as they discussed matters uppermost in their minds in the evenings after work. The two wives enjoyed spending time together also until Christmas 1954 when Marilou left for Quito for the birth of her second child.

Before that, in October, Jim wrote of his first wedding anniversary. "It has been the happiest and busiest year of my life." That happiness was crowned the following February when their daughter Valerie was born at Shell Mera in Nate and Marj Saint's house. Jim's parents arrived from Peru, where they had been staying with his brother, in order to see their grandchild. Jim was fascinated by his baby daughter and took every opportunity to pick her up for a cuddle. Later, after his parents had returned home, progress reports were mailed to them with loving details by the proud father. Bert and Colleen also visited them later on, making it a very rich year for family reunions and get-togethers.

Even with plenty of opportunities for socializing, Jim still forged ahead with the work of building, teaching, holiday baptismal classes and instructing young Indians so that they, in time, could take on the church organization and administration themselves. Translating the Scriptures took a good deal of effort and Jim also had to be prepared to set out on a mercy errand of healing any time an emergency arose.

Jim derived a great deal of satisfaction from their first, almost permanent, home, "First the tent, then the thatched roof in Puyupungu, and now boards, concrete, and aluminum!" Details of the new garden are lovingly written down in letters describing both the ornamental plants and the food crops. Many a time he must have felt thankful that his parents had taught their children to raise fruit and vegetables back in Portland. His artist's eye rejoiced in the profusion of colors among the flowers, and the pineapple, coffee, corn and avocados made welcome, yet economical, changes to the daily diet.

Only two adverse situations threatened their happiness. "The rain has set in suddenly again," Jim wrote in a letter home, thinking no doubt of all the trouble the floods had caused them in the past. Then—a more sinister note, "We have just learned of an Auca attack not far from Arajuno . . . the Aucas killed two children and their mother."

Would Jim and his fellow-missionaries be able to make a breakthrough to these savage tribespeople with the healing message of the Gospel? And, even more immediately urgent, would Ed and his little family be safe in Arajuno where they had taken up residence? Events had moved inexorably forward for some time. Plans for the individual missionary families dovetailed with remarkable precision. The overall blueprint for Operation Auca showed the touch of a Master's hand in its creation. "Man proposes but God disposes," and whatever critics might say in the future, the four young men involved felt supremely confident that they were moving forward in God's will.

Pete Fleming, after helping the McCullys to settle in at Shandia, had flown off to the United States to marry Olive. Eventually, after Jim and Elisabeth had moved back to Shandia with Pete's departure, Ed and Marilou had become sufficiently fluent in the Quichua language to contemplate a further move to an area so far unreached by the Gospel. Arajuno had presented an obviously suitable opportunity. Originally a small city with considerable amenities, set up by the Shell Company for the purpose of finding oil, it had been abandoned in 1949, and the jungle had been gradually encroaching over the houses, hotel and narrowgauge railway ever since. However, it was placed in a strategic area on the very edge of Auca territory and it seemed possible to make use of some of the building materials left behind.

After flying over with Nate several times, Ed felt sufficiently confident to build a small house, making use of the local materials. Significantly, though, a stout electric fence was erected about thirty yards from the house, beyond the limits of possible spears aimed in their direction.

Olive and Peter on their return settled in the house Jim built in Puyupungu. Roger Youderian and his wife Barbara, together with their two children, had originally come to Ecuador to work with the fierce Jivaro tribe. Nate Saint paid them frequent visits when he flew in with supplies to Macuma. Eventually Roger felt that his fellow missionary Frank Drown was quite able to maintain the station on his own and decided to move to Wambini, again possessing an air-strip, admittedly in poor shape, and some semi-derelict Shell Oil Company houses. With Nate's help, the flight in was accomplished and the family established in the hastily refurbished premises. By September 1955, however, the Youderians had moved back again to Macuma, although they were the last to be involved in the Auca project.

The five pioneer families were being drawn together by their common burning interest to take the Gospel to the Auca tribe. Like a spider's web, with Nate and Marj Saint in the center with their radio at Shell Mera, they were all linked by tenuous threads of communication.

Nate himself was the only one of the five having experienced any contact, albeit indirect, with the Aucas themselves. In his little yellow Piper plane he had flown over Auca territory many times but it was difficult to spot groups of a small tribe, numbering at the most a thousand members, in a vast area of densely wooded jungle. They were a byword for unexplained savagery, hating white men, people from other tribes and even killing their own kinsmen. All the young men were trained to become deadly marksmen with their lethal spears.

Naturally, although anxious to take the good news of Christ to these jungle folk, the five missionaries did their homework carefully, finding out as much as possible from first-hand accounts about their outlook on life and tribal habits before they made any overtures to them. Shell Oil men had been killed in the past by Aucas and although employers had tried to win their friendship by gifts left close by their houses, up to 1955 they had made no significant breakthrough. Although much criticism was levelled later at the five young men, they planned their strategy carefully, knowing full well the Aucas' murderous habits. Theirs was no sudden impulsive invasion of Auca territory without weighing up the possible cost and probable dangers first.

In September 1955, Ed and Nate at last spied, from the air, a cluster of Auca houses near Arajuno. From that moment they began a regular program of dropping gifts as a token of friendship, being unable to communicate more closely initially with any safety. Jim felt it was right to move forward, having met with a great deal of encouragement from his work in Shandia where a small group of believers now possessed a few Scriptures in their own language. With a strongly-built house, an airstrip and a base for a new school laid down, Jim had visions of establishing a similar nucleus eventually amongst the Aucas themselves. At what cost and how long it might take he had no idea. It was not a question of abandoning all he had done previously but it was his great desire that the work at Shandia might become autonomous and he kept training his band of converts to that end. The fact that Ed, Pete, Nate and Roger shared his vision to reach new frontiers confirmed to him that the Lord had brought them together to Ecuador for that very purpose.

"What do you think of an aerial survey?" Ed suggested to Nate one day. In such a dense forest region it was the only possible means of identifying Auca settlements. Foot slogging would produce few results besides placing them in greater danger. The five were concerned because all preliminary investigations had to be carried out in the utmost secrecy. They couldn't even alert their families and prayer-partners, although they especially needed to be covered by prayer for this project. Nate began to type up a diary of events and Jim committed more of his thoughts and plans to his journal.

It was not just for their own safety they feared. If other groups, who were not interested in missionary efforts but in finding out more about the Auca culture, heard of their plans they might blunder into the area in an aggressive way and cause bloodshed. Once alerted in this manner it could prove very difficult to establish any kind of friendly relationship with the Auca people.

Their only Auca contact was a woman, Dayuma, who had escaped some years previously after a tribal feud. She worked on the estate of Don Carlos who had lived on their territory for twenty-six years until he had to leave after many savage attacks.

Talking with him left them no illusions that the

Aucas would be an easy conquest. A victim of many raids, he recounted these stories willingly to put the five missionaries in the picture. Dayuma corroborated his evidence. "Do not trust them," she warned. "To you they might seem friendly for a while but they will not stop short of killing." At this stage they could well have been tempted to pull out of the whole enterprise but in a surprising way it made them all the more determined. "Savage stone-age killers who have never been reached by the Gospel before need the message of God's redeeming love more than many others," was Pete's sober conviction as he confided his impressions in his diary. In spite of the danger, in spite of the knowledge they had gained about the murderous character of the Aucas, "I have a quiet peace about it," he was able to write in all sincerity.

At this stage the five young men began working together in close harmony on Operation Auca, as they termed it. Although well known to each other, up to this time each had been responsible for his own particular area of work with Nate acting as link man, but from now on they would function as a team.

The first survey with Ed yielded the sight of about fifteen clearings and a few houses. They were not easily spotted and the two men had almost given up after flying for a long time and running low on fuel. About a fortnight later Nate had to take Jim and Pete over to Villano for a preaching campaign amongst the Quichua. Flying over Arajuno with Jim brought no results but on the second trip with Pete over a slightly different route they observed some signs of clearings only a quarter of an hour's flight from Ed's house. Coaxing the guides that were with them to keep silence about their sightings, they began to plan their future strategy.

Probably the most immediate pressing problem was that of language. Without being able to communicate with them, it would be extremely difficult to get across their message of peace and goodwill merely by gestures and sundry gifts. With this in mind, Jim hiked the four-hour trail to Don Carlos' estate with the purpose of chatting to Dayuma. He picked up many useful phrases from her and wrote them down carefully in his notebook. Even though she herself had been a victim of Auca savagery and had every reason to hate them, he took no chances. He did not divulge to her the reason for his interest in the Auca tongue.

Even on his return the program of dropping gifts could not begin until rehearsals had taken place to ensure everything went without a hitch. Two of the wives helped with adjusting weights and marking their release. Nate confessed to an attack of butterflies in the tummy, he attached so much importance to this new development. Yet at the same time he felt confident that the Lord was more than equal to the situation.

Jim and Nate finally experienced the thrill of seeing their first gift dropped on target, a new machete, carefully wrapped up in canvas sacking so the Aucas would not cut themselves on it. What is more, an Auca man walked out to investigate the bundle and then waved it above his head. The plan was to plant the gifts in different spots so that no-one would think that they were favoring one particular house. Other gifts followed when flying was possible.

Finding out that a group of Aucas regularly lay hidden in a spot near Ed's house covered by thick undergrowth to spy out what was happening, the missionaries decided to make a model of a plane decorated with ribbon streamers and hang it up outside the McCullys' house. In this way they would connect Ed with the enterprise. From this moment there was no turning back. Drop after drop followed at irregular intervals with more response from the Indians.

# 11

Meanwhile Jim memorized the few Auca phrases he had written down. His total commitment became obvious to Elisabeth and she began to question the timing. Was it really God's moment to go forward? What would happen to the work already established in Shandia? And when would the school building be finished?

Jim had no such inhibitions. "I am called," was his simple response to Elisabeth's query. It wasn't that Jim was tired of life and intent on throwing it away carelessly. On the contrary he had everything going for him—health, strength, a happy marriage and a lovely little baby daughter. "You'd love her now," he wrote to his parents. "She surely does leave us without any leisure for ourselves except after supper, and we love it."

The whole campaign was carefully planned and monitored. There would be those afterwards who would complain that lives had been sacrificed needlessly. True, there was always an element of risk but Jim was well aware of this, making what he thought was adequate compensation for it. But if the Lord called in a certain direction, he would follow. Elisabeth, speaking about events more than thirty years afterwards stated unequivocally, "Jim Elliot considered himself disposable," and that just about summed it up.

Although Elisabeth entertained doubts about it being the right moment to advance, she fully supported Jim in his plans. She got hold of some more linguistic material to add to his and they discussed moving into a tribe together as soon as friendly communications had been set up. Yet Jim had a great sense of responsibility towards the Indians with whom he had been working. It wasn't just a question of forsaking routine jobs for the excitement of making contact with the Aucas. While he was waiting for favorable weather for flights, he carried on with constructing a new school, Bible studies with young fellows, and attempting to finish off a translation of Luke's Gospel.

Other trips followed with encouraging results. When, for the first time, Nate's plane dived low, the Aucas scattered rapidly in fear. Gradually, the tribal people became accustomed to them and clustered round avidly to seize the gifts as they were dropped. Emboldened by their success, Jim and Ed began to call out phrases, "I like you, I am your friend!" which they had learned from Dayuma. Not all the five were of one mind about what steps to take next. Some felt that they should progress cautiously and concentrate on learning more Auca phrases and setting up another airstrip before making ground contact with the Aucas. "They're still stone-age killers," argued Pete. "It's unlikely they'll lose their centuries-old hatred of white people in a few weeks."

Yet they were spurred on by fresh signs of hope. Up to that time Roger Youderian had been passing through a particularly black period in his life, making up his mind to leave the mission field because he "hadn't measured up to God's standards." When approached by Nate to join the team he was still undecided, but finally he received a clear sense of direction from God and unreservedly committed himself to the Auca cause.

Another heartening fact was that the Aucas were beginning to tie gifts, such as headbands of brightly colored feathers, for the missionaries on the dropping line. Occasionally one of the tribespeople would wave to them in return as they swooped over the clearings, and they noticed with excitement that one or two Aucas were sporting gifts of clothing let down to them from the plane like T-shirts and trousers. Ed commented in his diary, "It is time we were getting closer to them on the ground," and he began to plan the next moves forward in the campaign. There was certainly more need for urgency now that their secret was out. In spite of their precautions, local Indians chatted openly about their sorties over Auca territory. It was only a matter of time before other less well-intentioned groups forced their way in.

"Terminal City" was the code name given to the largest collections of Auca houses grouped in a rough, village formation. Nate and his crew continued to make regular trips over there, swooping down lower as they gained confidence. More goods were dropped out of the plane which were now quickly picked up by the Aucas. Ed took closeup snaps of the five missionaries which he planned to enlarge and drop down so that they would be easily recognized when they came to a face-to-face encounter on the ground.

By early December their plans were formulated. A shelter would be erected on the strip of river beach selected by them for landing the plane. Then they would keep a low profile until the natives had accepted their presence, after which they would venture out and try to make friendly overtures to them. The landing strip went by the exotic name of Palm Beach and it took some finding. They needed a sufficiently long run, clear of trees and large boulders, situated reasonably close to the Auca village, and at first they could only survey it from the air. The river twisted and turned rather acutely but at last they saw a possible landing place which could be improved by the removal of a few trees when the men had landed with their tools. Otherwise the passage might prove slightly narrow for the plane.

They planned to make a tree-house and stock it with sufficient supplies for several days. Being realistic, all five agreed it was necessary to take firearms for an emergency but they would be kept very much in the background. Should things go seriously wrong, there remained the two escape routes of rafts on the river or a rescue by plane. In spite of their enthusiasm, they were determined not to take foolish risks and to provide for every eventuality. All the same, they didn't really expect any insuperable obstacles. "We believe in a short time we shall have the privilege of meeting these fellows with the story of the Grace of God," wrote Nate after a working lunch with Ed and Marilou.

Later it was Marilou who, in the seventh month of her pregnancy, when Ed was away at a conference at Puyupungu, courageously walked down the garden path at the news that a naked Auca with a lance had been spotted nearby. In her hands she took gifts, calling out, "I like you." Fermin, the Indian guard, was convinced she had gone crazy when she refused to give him a gun and ammunition. No traces of the man except a footprint were found but it put everyone on alert from that time onward.

Again it was Marilou who made a tremendous effort to provide a traditional Christmas for their guests, the Flemings and the Elliots. Improvised decorations and a bamboo tree brightened up their small home and while everyone entered into the festivities, the men were tense like tightly wound springs. One evening the wives got together and discussed the possibility of becoming widows. It had to be faced yet not one thought of putting pressure on her husband to withdraw from the enterprise.

Tuesday, January 3, 1956, was the date set to start Operation Auca. The previous day Nate intended to transport the Flemings and McCullys back to Arajuno. Over the morning radio call he asked Jim to be ready also. Conditions were ideal for flying and Nate felt they could make use of the extra time for going over plans together. Jim tossed into his luggage any items he thought might be of interest to the Aucas. Clutching them and other essential bits of equipment, he kissed Elisabeth goodbye and climbed into the plane.

There was no looking back. Jim had no intention of throwing away his life in a dramatic gesture but he had weighed the risks and still felt wholeheartedly committed. Like a knight sworn to follow his liege lord he went forward to battle against ignorance and evil. In a last letter to his father, five days before he flew to Palm Beach with Nate, he warned his parents, " . . . they have never had any contact with white man other than killing. They have no word for God in their language, only for devils and spirits. I know you will pray." Elisabeth watched the plane until it disappeared. Would she ever see him again?

That night at Arajuno the five men checked items of equipment and discussed final plans. Nate was the last to fall asleep. Writing in his diary he confessed to mulling over his problems in the dark. On him lay the main responsibility, and oblivion was a long time in coming and then only lasted for a short while.

A quick repair to a minor problem with the plane, then loading followed by breakfast filled the first hour of Day 1. After prayer together, the five fellows broke spontaneously into the hymn which had become a favorite with them all, "We rest on Thee, our Shield and our Defender." The last line, "Victors, we rest with Thee through endless days," was shortly to hold a new significance for them, though none could have foreseen that as they sang on that January morning. Radio contact had already been made with Marj, and morale was high as they prepared for the first experimental flight although they knew, and none more so than Nate, that they could encounter a host of difficulties. Theoretically, a landing on the narrow strip was possible but they still had to put their theory into practice. What if the plane were damaged extensively and the two men were stranded on the bank at the mercy of the Aucas?

A thick river fog shrouded the area at first but they were able to dive underneath and make a landing on the second run in. Getting airborne again was a tougher proposition, but having unloaded the equipment, Nate took off once more, with a good deal of help from Ed, who also recorded the flight on his movie camera. Sobered by the experience, and the problems involved, he changed his plans for the second trip and just flew in Jim and Roj with basic necessities. In all, Nate made five trips and then flew over Terminal City with a message for the Aucas, "Come to the river tomorrow." Meanwhile the other three had lost no time in fixing up a primitive ladder and tree house in spite of the attentions of swarms of biting insects. "Bugs are bad," commented Ed in the note he sent next morning via Nate to Marilou, with a request for insect repellant among a list of other necessities.

In Jim's letter to Elisabeth, he assured her, "We had a good night . . . didn't set a watch . . . as we feel really cozy and secure thirty-five feet off the ground in our little bunks." Nate and Pete flew in and were relieved to get the radio-transmitter functioning again so they could call Marj in Shell Mera. On Thursday's flight they were heartened to see human footprints beside animal tracks. The three men at base camp treated the news with good-humored ridicule at first but when Jim and Roj set off to check the information on foot they were encouraged when their sightings were confirmed.

In spite of the very obvious dangers of their situation, the mood on the beach was relaxed. Nate commented, "Except for forty-seven billion flying insects of every sort, this place is a little paradise." Later Jim started to read them a novel. "We roared over even remotely funny suggestions and skipped to the end to see who married whom!" Nate made a further flight over Terminal City to persuade the inhabitants to visit the river settlement and saw a man pointing with both hands in that direction. Elated by the meaning behind the gesture, Nate was not even then to be lulled into a false sense of security. "We must not let that lead us to carelessness. It is no small thing to try to bridge between the twentieth century and the Stone Age."

Friday started just like other days on the beach with the men spread out over the area and Ed calling Auca phrases in the direction of the jungle. Although they had prayed for a positive reaction to their invitation, all were momentarily transfixed when a male voice replied from across the river. A man and two females came into view wearing only strings round the waist, wrist and thighs. Recovering their equilibrium, the five gave a shout of welcome.

Jim, stripped to his shorts, started to wade across the river to them, holding out his hands to lead them back. Using all the Auca phrases they had at their disposal, the missionaries tried to reassure them that their intentions were purely friendly. Reinforcing their talk with gifts of knives, a machete and a model plane, they began to allay the Aucas' suspicions. One of the five disappeared discreetly to camouflage their guns, which they had brought as an emergency precaution, while the others took photographs, produced magazines for them to inspect and even sprayed the man with insect repellant to offer him instant relief from the irritating hordes of stinging pests.

As the man showed marked interest in the plane, they put a shirt on him to protect him from the cold at a higher altitude and took him for a short flight over Terminal City. Far from being overawed by this miracle of modern science, "George" leaned out to wave and yell at his people on the ground below. On their safe return, the five men gave thanks to God with an open demonstration that they were speaking to a supreme being. Then they plied their guests with refreshments which, although completely strange to them, they obviously enjoyed. However, they showed no enthusiasm when the five men mimed the message that they would like to visit their Auca village.

# 12

A puzzling reaction—what did it indicate? The fellows tried to show "George" how an airstrip should be made in their village using sticks to represent trees and one of their model planes. "Delilah" appeared impatient and she was the first to disappear down the beach when Nate and Pete prepared to leave. "George" was ready to step into the plane again but they had to leave without him, stacking their cans of exposed film carefully inside.

"George" trailed after "Delilah" into the forest but the older woman squatted most of the night by the campfire. By the misty half-light of early dawn when Jim climbed down the ladder from the tree-house, the embers were still glowing. This could only be a good sign. They must be gaining the Aucas' confidence, they argued, and this new day, Saturday, could only bring them even better results to help them achieve their goal. Relations, albeit tenuous, had been established. Surely the Aucas would soon return to invite them back to their village.

Slowly the hours ticked away—nine, ten, eleven. The men busied themselves over various preparations and tasks but their eyes kept straying to the gap in the clearing across the river where they expected the Aucas to re-emerge. By noon Jim decided on action. Prudently he refrained from crossing the river on his own but he explored an old forest trail which, however, yielded only tracks of animals but no human footprints. On a trial flight over Terminal City, Nate and Pete were disturbed to note reactions of fear. After throwing down gifts, George appeared, and by the third trip George and another young Auca fellow were returning their smiles. This could only promise good for the future, they reasoned. After all, it had been only a few days.

Ed's mood in a note to Marilou appeared cautiously optimistic, "We believe they'll arrive, if not tonight, then early tomorrow ... we feel now we ought to press going over there and get the airstrip in as fast as possible—but we'll have to wait and see how God leads us, and them, too." Pete and Nate delivered this note in Arajuno that evening.

With the return flight on Sunday morning Marilou included some ice cream and warm blueberry muffins. With extras like this to their diet in addition to the dishes they prepared for themselves in their improvised kitchen at the base of the tree-house, they fared well. As Ed remarked to Marilou, in the same note, "This has been a well-fed operation from start to end." Roj had experimented with scrap materials to build a functional though primitive stove and Jim had contributed fish he had caught to vary the menu sometimes.

Each of the five men had pulled his weight in "Operation Auca." True, Nate and Pete escaped sometimes to the comparative civilization of Arajuno, but on them lay the heavy responsibility of landing on a very inadequate airstrip and then getting the plane airborne again with a minimum margin of safety. Contact with base was imperative, they all agreed. Fresh supplies of goods and equipment were required on Palm Beach. On the return trip they took back written notes and completed cans of movie film. If anything adverse did happen to them, they were determined that the whole enterprise should be well-documented for posterity. Others who might take over the job later would benefit both from their mistakes and their expertise.

"Pray. I believe today's the day," called Pete, waving goodbye to the wives at Arajuno as he boarded the plane. An almost identical message, "Pray for us. This is the day!" was beamed across the radio to Marj at Shell Mera just after noon by Nate. Flying over Terminal City earlier, he had noticed only a few women and children. This could only mean that a deputation of older men was on its way to the river site. "Will contact you next at four-thirty," he promised Marj, expecting to have great news for her.

The story of those next few hours on the beach can only be pieced together by conjecture. At Shell Mera, Marj and Olive waited anxiously with no reassuring information to pass on to Marilou and Barbara when they phoned through. It wasn't until the next day that Elisabeth became aware that plans had possibly misfired. Marj had refrained from contacting her overnight, unwilling to cause a panic if nothing unfavorable had happened. "Stand by at ten o'clock for Johnny's report, would you please." (Johnny Kernan was the auxiliary pilot who worked with Nate.)

His message, relayed by Marj to Shandia, brought no comfort. "The plane's fabric has been stripped off but there's no sign of our husbands."

The news could no longer be contained. From radio station HCJB the word went out, "Five men missing in Auca territory." Marilou, although she had been flown with Barbara to Shell Mera, felt reluctant to stay there long. Both were convinced that there would be some survivors so she returned. It wasn't until Tuesday that three of the women met together, Elisabeth being accompanied by Nate's sister Rachel. Sighting of a fire upstream by an Ecuadorian airline pilot raised hopes again. Could it be one of Nate's signal flares? But these hopes were soon dashed by Marj's news that Johnny had seen a body clothed in khaki pants and a white T-shirt floating in the river.

A search party had already been organized led by Frank Drown, Roger's missionary colleague. The United States Air Rescue Service in Panama were notified. Marilou, back at Arajuno, prepared food for the men before they set out. Quichua porters were naturally apprehensive of joining the team. They knew too much about the Aucas already and their unpredictable savage attacks. Frank was chosen because of his familiarity with the terrain, although he personally had worked largely with the Jivaros. An American doctor and thirteen Ecuadorian soldiers volunteered to join the expedition.

"All for now. Your lover, Jim." These were the last words that Jim wrote in a quick note to Elisabeth, which Nate and Pete had handed to her earlier in the week. Just seven days later, together with the other three wives, she learned the news that one body had been found. On a fourth flight over Palm Beach, Johnny had radioed Marj with the information. From the description of the clothing Barbara was sure it couldn't have been Roj.

United States Air Force planes from Panama had already landed at Arajuno, the largest airstrip in the area, to help with the search. Just after the party left the radio came alive again. "Another body sighted," was the somber message that Johnny passed on to Marj. At this stage no positive identification was possible so the wives were left in ignorance as to whose bodies they might turn out to be. With deep conviction, Marilou had already made a statement to a member of the search party, "There is no hope. All the men are dead," but they longed to know details of the probable massacre. Meanwhile, "His grace was sufficient," commented Elisabeth simply.

After camping for the night, the search party pressed forward again Thursday morning, committing their sad and emotionally painful enterprise to the Lord. They prayed for a safe passage for themselves through Auca territory and definite proof of the fate of the five missionaries. Johnny took off in another flight. He made contact with Frank Drown of the search party by two-way radio passing on the news that canoes of Quichuas from Ed's station at Arajuno had paddled through to Palm Beach on their own initiative. "One of the Indians who was a believer came across Ed's body on the beach and he's removed Ed's watch." One killed for sure, but what about the fate of the other four? Hopes of survival were waning, but could two or three have escaped and be hiding wounded in the dense Equatorial forest? Speed was imperative at this stage. Four full days had elapsed since the last radio contact. If alive, they would be in urgent need of medical attention and food.

Providentially, in spite of the tension, many duties claimed the missionary wives' attention. Routine chores had to be attended to, meals prepared which no one felt very much like eating, and babies tended. Everyone tried to preserve a semblance of calm for the sake of the children, but it was difficult with so many people coming and going.

In the afternoon the flight out from Shell Mera was an impressive sight. Highest of all were the Air Rescue Service with U.S. Navy planes below. Sandwiched between them and Johnny Kernan's yellow Piper (a twin of Nate's aircraft) was an army helicopter. Its occupant, Major Nurnberg, landed briefly twice, the second time on Palm Beach, and then hovered as low as possible over the muddy water of the river, seeking for positive clues.

On his return, Marilou was flown in from Arajuno and after a conference of the military personnel, the wives themselves asked for a frank and free discussion of details. They did not wish to be shielded from the truth, however stark, and finally Nurnberg told them, "Four bodies have been sighted. At this stage identification is not possible but one had on a red belt of woven material."

"That's Pete," said Olive.

Barbara Youderian also knew for certain that Roj had met his death because he was the only one clothed in a T-shirt and blue jeans. What was unclear was whether Ed's body had been one of the four in the river. Could one of the men have possibly escaped? A forlorn and unlikely hope, but all the wives received the news with calm and a sense of acceptance. "The Lord has closed our hearts to grief and hysteria, and filled in with His perfect peace."

The search party on foot had been informed by radio that four of the missionaries were dead. Thursday night they camped again near Auca territory but Frank Drown knew he had to face the unpleasant task of identifying the remains and preparing a hasty burial for them. They reached the beach on Friday morning after an early start, fearful of possible attacks en route from Aucas lying in wait. They divided into groups, examining the wreckage and searching for clues, but it was the helicopter crew, when they flew in later, who pointed them to the bodies in the water. Four bodies were towed in by canoe and laid face down on the beach but Ed's was not among them. Mercifully, his had been recognized by the Indians the previous day so none of the wives was left in anxious suspense about the fate of her husband.

A *Life* magazine photographer, Cornell Capa, was dropped on the beach by helicopter to record the last glimpses of the five martyrs—martyrs in the fullest sense of the word for they had not only been killed for their faith, but by the manner of their dying had witnessed to the whole world the all-embracing love of God. A tropical rain storm blew up as the bodies were carried across on aluminum sheets from the tree-house and hastily dropped into the communal grave. Torrents of rain and the uncanny half-light set the scene as Indians filled in the hole and fellow-missionaries offered up a brief prayer. Then "Let's go," said Major Nurnberg, still covering them with his gun to avoid another possible attack by the Aucas. Knowing there remained no other possible task that they could perform for their comrades, the ground party climbed into the canoe with Capa, while his exposed film was loaded into the helicopter.

Traveling in the over-crowded canoes was fraught with danger. Stiff and soaked through, Cornell felt mightily relieved to climb out for an overnight camp and eat a meal the missionaries had prepared. No chances were being taken even at this stage. A guard was posted all round the area. It had been established from examining the four bodies that the men had died from lance wounds and no one wished to become a new target for these deadly weapons. Round the campfire Don Johnson, one of the missionaries, thanked the Lord for a safe and successful mission so far. Then he gave thanks also for the lives of those five men, each a different character but all imbued with the same spirit of love and self-sacrifice.

Of all the tributes which would be given to them in the weeks ahead, this had surely been the most meaningful. It came straight from the heart of one who had known and loved them—not a polished eulogy but a simple appreciation of their lives and service to the Lord. The river raged through the night and sounds of exotic birds and animals penetrated the thick jungle. No one slept much and they were glad to move off again at dawn.

Palm Beach was to be visited once more, this time by the five wives who had been invited by Captain De Witt of the Rescue Service to see their husbands' communal grave. Kneeling on the floor of the plane, they glimpsed the strip of sand, in stark contrast to the verdant green of the jungle on one side and the muddy waters of the Curaray on the other. It represented a peaceful scene in the morning sunlight compared with the violent action which had erupted there a fortnight before. Marj Saint spoke for them all when she commented, "That is the most beautiful little cemetery in the world."

"They were lovely and pleasant in their lives and in their deaths they were not divided,"—words poured out in anguish from David's heart over 3,000 years ago when he learned of the death of his best friend Jonathan, slain in battle against the Philistines together with his father Saul—words which could be equally applied to these five young men, cut off in the flower of their youth. Yet they had faced up to this very possibility long before they had set out on their final venture, weighed the cost and counted it nothing compared with the joy of carrying out one of our Lord's final injunctions to his disciples, "Go ye therefore, and teach all nations, baptizing them in the name of the Father, and the Son, and of the Holy Ghost . . ." (Matt. 28:19).

# *Epilogue*

The search party would gladly have spared the widows any further emotional stress when they returned to Shell Mera two days later. But all five insisted on being told as many details as possible, having only just learned a few basic facts from the flight crew. It was out of no sense of morbid curiosity but a genuine and understandable desire to reconstruct the last few hours of their husbands' lives.

Mercifully, no one was left in doubt. Watches, notebooks and wedding rings were produced by the members of the expedition, positive proof of identity for each of the widows. Without being able to come to any final conclusion, they discussed the evident ugly marks of violence, multiple lance marks on the bodies and the almost total disintegration of the plane. Where were the guns that the missionaries had been so careful to take in with their equipment? How was it that no one had escaped, that no one had been able to reach the plane or even alert the outside world by radio? The most likely explanation seemed to be that the approaching party of Aucas from Terminal City had deliberately moved in, ostentatiously to respond to their overtures of friendship, while another even larger force had crept up secretly through the jungle to take the missionaries off their guard.

No final conclusion could be reached at this stage. Too little was yet known about the Auca mentality and way of viewing life which would explain the sudden attack on white men who had offered nothing but gifts and friendship. The wives couldn't help wondering, "Did my husband suffer long? And did he think about me and his family as he fell?" Private grief was not allowed to surface because of the children, but it would have been strange if it had not existed at all. Yet with this personal sense of loss there was a calmness and acceptance devoid of bitterness.

It would have been the easiest thing in the world to abandon the whole project, leave the area and put as much distance as possible between themselves and the arena of tragedy. Everyone would have forgiven them for doing just that. Yet all the wives had felt as committed as their husbands. Their deaths merely meant that the wives would step into their shoes.

Marilou had a very valid excuse for flying to the States soon after the massacre. It was there that her third son was born, but she returned to Ecuador a little while afterward to work in Quito with Marj Saint at the missionary headquarters. The two wives had six children to care for between them. Barbara Youderian with her two small children returned to the Jivaro tribe, and Betty with Valerie, now ten months old, traveled back to Shandia. Olive Fleming took longer to reach a decision as she had only lived in the jungle with Pete for two months, but she was

just as anxious as the other four to carry out the will
of God. Hobey Lawrance was dispatched with his
family to Shell Mera by Missionary Aviation Fellowship as a replacement for Nate Saint.

Rachel, Nate's sister, carried on with language
study, using Dayuma, the Auca woman who worked
on the nearby estate. Flights were resumed over Auca
territory with gift drops. Elisabeth had much to encourage her with the new sense of commitment and
responsibility among the Indians at Shandia following Jim's death. She taught in the school set up by
Jim and Pete Fleming but also did a little medical
work and carried on with her translation of parts of
the Bible into the Quichua language. Messages of
sympathy continued to pour in, often from people
whose lives had been completely changed by the
death of the five men, who on hearing the story of the
martyrdom had reappraised their own lives and ex-
amined their standing before God. There were also
letters from critics and cranks, but the former far out-
weighed the latter.

People also marveled at Elisabeth's willingness to
remain near the Aucas with her baby daughter, possibly risking their lives as well. Elisabeth's trust in
the Lord remained implicit in spite of the tragic
events. "Where I go, Valerie goes. I believe the Lord
expects me to be as careful as possible about Valerie's
health in our home, but when I accept the hospitality
from the Indians, I trust the Lord to take care of the
results."

A further development which changed the course
of events again was the emergence of two Auca
women from the jungle roughly a year later. Elisabeth

took them into her home at Shandia. Eventually she, Valerie and Rachel lived with the Aucas for almost a year on their territory before returning with her written material and photographs. During the course of that year, with patience and perseverance, more details were discovered about the events leading up to the massacre on the beach. Some of the tribespeople had taken the part of the foreigners. In *The Dayuma Story*, Ethel Wallis recounted how Mintaka had said enthusiastically, "They were good foreigners, they laughed a lot." She also added that there were others who disagreed, "If we don't kill them they will surely kill us and eat us. There were only five of them now but more may come. They might kill us all."

Malcolm's tribute in *Macbeth* would make a fitting epitaph to Jim Elliot and also to his four colleagues.

> Nothing in his life
> Became him like the leaving of it; he died
> As one that had been studied in his death
> To throw away the dearest thing he owned
> As 'twere a careless trifle.

Jim wrote down his own philosophy of life-and-death in one of his well-worn notebooks in 1948. "God, I pray Thee, light these idle sticks of my life and may I burn for Thee. Consume my life, my God, for it is Thine. I seek not a long life, but a full one, like you, Lord Jesus."